The REFLECTIVE EXECUTIVE

other books by Emilie Griffin

TURNING
Reflections on the Experience of Conversion

CLINGING
The Experience of Prayer

CHASING THE KINGDOM
A Parable of Faith

EMILIE GRIFFIN

The REFLECTIVE EXECUTIVE

A Spirituality of Business and Enterprise

• • • • •

CROSSROAD • NEW YORK

1993

The Crossroad Publishing Company
370 Lexington Avenue, New York NY 10017

All Scripture quotations are from the Jerusalem Bible unless otherwise indicated.

Printed in the United States of America

Library of Congress Cataloging-in-Publication Data

Griffin, Emilie.
The reflective executive : a spirituality of business and enterprise / Emilie Griffin.
p. cm.
Includes bibliographical references.
ISBN 0-8245-1271-5
1. Management—Religious aspects—Christianity. 2. Spiritual life. 3. Christian life—1960- I. Title.
HD38.G729 1993
658.4'094—dc20 93-13913
CIP

Grateful acknowledgment is made for permission to quote the following material:

"Dawn" from *Poet in New York* by Frederico García Lorca, translated by Greg Simon and Steven F. White, edited and with an introduction and notes by Christopher Maurer. Farrar, Straus and Giroux, copyright © 1988. Used by permission.

"Potholes" by Thulani David, copyright © 1985 by Thulani Davis, from *Playing the Changes*. Wesleyan University Press. Used with permission.

for my mother
Helen Russell Dietrich
and my grandmother
Lucy Powell Russell
mentors in spirituality and enterprise
and for my father-in-law
Henry Francis Griffin I
who believed in Wall Street

CONTENTS

TO THE READER

I remember, somewhat, how I crossed over the thin rope bridge between the creative arts and commerce. What day it was I can't remember, but something about my first visit to New York, at nineteen, laid open for me a vision of that city as a pulsating center of life, teeming with hope and opportunity. Later on—when it was I scarcely know—I began to bridge another gap: the seeming chasm between faith-experience and the marketplace.

If God is one, if God is loving, if God is everywhere, why this gap? In fact, the gap is within us, in our divided hearts, in our splintered understanding. This book—and the talks and lectures that have given rise to it—are meant as simple faith-statements. In these chapters I mean to express a whole, unified vision of who we are in God's sight and what we can become.

In November 1989 I was invited to speak to a new group of managers and leaders, called together as the Business Vocation Conference. In that setting I was able to learn—all at once, and most surprisingly—how many others shared the vision I was there to express.

Since that eventful meeting in Chicago, the group has evolved into a focused national effort under the auspices of the Woodstock Theological Center in Washington. To all those in this significant enterprise I say thanks. I'm especially grateful for encouragements from Thomas Bausch, dean of the Business School at Marquette University; James Connor, S.J., of Woodstock; Michael Flynn, now national director of the conference; Arthur Gray, president of Dreyfus Personal Management; John Haughey, S.J., and Father John Langan, S.J., thinkers and writers whose work is extensive and influential; John Stollenwerk, who heads the Allyn-Edmonds Shoe Company; and Joseph Sciortino of SYSCO, Inc., in Florida. Frank Butler of FADICA (Foundations and Donors Interested in Catholic Activities, Washington) has been a strong friend and resource.

To many in the National Center for the Laity—among them Clyde Evans, John Fontana, John McDermott, Greg Pierce, and Peggy Steinfels in particular—I say thanks. Their remarkable effort to encourage faith in the marketplace is, I think, different in character from other lay movements. This long-established group is good at celebrating grace in our everyday lives.

Since 1970 I have read Peter Drucker's book *The Effective Executive* often. For me this book has the force of a meditation. Between the lines in Drucker's book I find a spirituality of executive life, a faith-level not spoken aloud but still accessible. His clarity and reasonableness have been, from time to time, as strengthening to me as the Psalms.

During the 1980s I read widely in theology and looked for clues in the work of scholars to the puzzles of executive life. Among many fine teachers who have encouraged me in this process I need especially to mention Stephen J. Duffy, whose grasp of the ideas of Karl Rahner and of Paul Ricoeur have affected the flow of my thought.

Out of such sources, and my own thirty years in executive life, this book has been imagined and written. My hope is that you will find in it experience, strength, and hope for the challenges of the marketplace.

Emilie Griffin

New Orleans

1

EFFECTIVENESS

Cities are metaphors of consciousness. In and through them we see visions and dream dreams. In New York, Chicago, and London, massive economic power is felt in the roar of traffic, the howl of machinery, the tuning-fork vibrations of bridges, and the moan of tugs and barges. In search of fulfillment we rush down into subways, jounce to and from appointments on jarring, crowded buses, run to hail cabs, hurtle to airports, check in, rush to board, and wait on runways while frustrations mount. Disenchantment seizes us. Discouragement sets in. What, we wonder, are we living for? What path are we following? Sometimes, because of our disenchantment, we become more open to reminders of a simpler way. Whirrings of clock towers and sounds of church bells—even in the heart of the metropolis—call us to reflection and inwardness. Is God with us in the marketplace? Or must we executives leave our posts in order to experience faith?

From my first office in New York City, on the thirty-seventh floor of a Fifth Avenue tower, I could look down on St. Patrick's Cathedral. It looked like a child's plaything, a toy cathedral that I could lift and carry somewhere. Something about this troubled me. Cathedrals, I felt, should be looked up to. Later, when I visited England, I saw how cathedrals can dominate landscapes. Then I understood the new power balance of twentieth-century life. Lever House and the Seagram's Building, I concluded, are our new cathedrals. The Chrysler Building and the Empire State Building are our statements of value. Dwarfing the little churches on Park Avenue and Wall Street, they have created a new ethos. These buildings are proclamations of power.

We know that power corrupts. We do well to be wary of exalting power as power. Yet in candor we should also confess that these giants of the metropolis bear witness to our dreams. The naïve beauty of these sleek, upward-soaring towers is meant to lift us up. From their new heights and vantage points we can see whole valleys and rivers stretching before us, an ocean at our feet. In these and other dazzling ways, cities embody a vision.

They are fueled by our energies, drives that are clues to God's creative power working within us. Only because of the specks in our eyes do we say that in secular matters God is absent. The truth is otherwise. Faith tells us that our God is in charge of all endeavor. Our God works everywhere.

The presence of God in daily affairs was known to the ancient Hebrews as *Shekinah*, an intense, fiery perception of holiness seen not with the naked eye but with the inner eye. Closer to our own times, new mystics, persons of learning and prayer, have seen God's presence in the world. The poet Gerard Manley Hopkins tells us that the world is charged with the grandeur of God. "It will flame out, like shining from shook foil." Another mystic, the philosopher-scientist Pierre Teilhard de Chardin, speaks to us of (jarring phrase!) *holy matter*. From clues such as these we take courage. Possibly we will also be able to grasp God's presence in the marketplace.

Perhaps, however, a healing must come first. Our blindness must be taken away, our eyes must be transformed. A curious ailment afflicts us, a terrible double-mindedness that thinks some things are pure and others impure. These things are matters of faith; *those* are matters for the world. We are trapped in a habit of mind that conceives of business as unholy. This unholiness in the marketplace, it seems, is a prophecy that generally comes true. Where shall we go to escape this division in our lives, this gap in our understanding?

The flaw is not in God but in us. Once again we need to ask for a fresh burst of grace. When we left God out of our daily struggle, thinking we could manage without his help, when we set our agendas without him, when we built our businesses on something less than prayer, we took the chance that we would fail on the deepest possible level. When we forgot the faith of our childhood and set out to achieve things *by ourselves,* things that were either beneath God's notice or too worldly for his consideration, we made a foolish mistake. [How, precisely, in any given deal, were we planning to cut the Lord out? How, exactly, did we plan to slip things by him? Were we planning not to invite him to the meetings? Not to share the figures with him till we got things a bit farther along? Not to ask his advice because he is so overcontrolling? Were we planning to exclude him because our plans are so early-on, we don't need help? Do we, on the other hand, suppose that our projects are too small to interest him? Have we forgotten that this is the Lord who cares about the sparrow? Don't we know that this is the Lord who sees fit to forgive escalating debts?] My own sense is that we fail to include God not deliberately but through neglect. We don't so much exclude him as overlook his presence in the marketplace. God is the awkward, unfashionable outsider, the unwelcome guest. His dress is not contemporary; he is oblivious to the latest style. In our mind-picture he is painted by Michelangelo. All very well for the nineteenth century, but it will not do for us.

Intimacy with God is the simple truth that earlier, more hopeful generations knew. Prayer, unself-conscious friendship with God, is the stuff from which they once shaped businesses, skyscrapers, cities, and nations. Now the question nags at us. Where will we find this new power of vision, to see God in the marketplace?

Manhattan's towers rise as a clear sign of hope for the heroine of the film *Working Girl* as she rides the Staten Island ferry to her menial job on Wall Street. Director Mike Nichols speaks with wit and irony in this contemporary fairy tale, no more than a Horatio Alger story turned inside out. What enlightens us in the film, however, is neither the story nor its message, but Manhattan itself: civilization itself. That image of the metropolis, the skyline of lower Manhattan, rising in sunlight as the camera plunges across New York harbor, is a city seen in dreams, an image of perfection and desire. That picture stays with us long after the rest of the film has faded away.

The bright vision is underscored with a nearly biblical message. Carly Simon sings God's *fiat*, she asks creation to be. She asks rivers to run, dreamers to wake the nation. She heralds the sight of cities bathed in morning light. Sons and daughters of the morning arise. They are filled with hope and longing. The imagery is both American and biblical. If Nichols meant to be ironic, his irony has been swamped with deeper, archetypal meaning. For anyone conversant with Scripture the meaning is clear. What is revealed in the marketplace is a mystical vision: that of the New Jerusalem. Looking with secular eyes, one sees nothing more than steel and concrete, trash-filled streets, escalating poverty and homelessness, society out of control. But with eyes transformed by a biblical vision, one can see the face of God through the power of Manhattan, the splendor of the East River, Hudson, Harlem, in the singing bridges, the haze over Brooklyn and Queens. The metaphor of the metropolis, be it London or Chicago or Detroit, whether the vastness of Los Angeles or Miami, shows God present in ways seen only with the eyes of faith. Silver cities rise. Your sons and daughters sing the greatest song.

God is here! He is actually present! It is not beneath him to dwell on the Staten Island ferry, heading for Lower Manhattan. He is willing to descend with us into the underground chambers of the subway, to be with us in discomfort, boredom, alienation. He accompanies us to the boardroom. He attends the year-end meeting. In the community formed by us, by colleagues, by purchasers, buyers and sellers, customers satisfied and unsatisfied, he is present, bearing our sorrows, acquainted with grief.

What a contrast to our common way of thinking: that business, which is by its very nature materialistic, somehow has to be spiritualized. The reality is otherwise. It is our mistake to think that we will somehow take business, which is unholy, and by some sacrifice or offering, make it holy. That tragic mistake is the crucial error we must expose. To correct this false notion we need not only action but contemplation.

Contemplation is the radical work of the marketplace. Reflection is our passage to reality, to a new understanding, a different consciousness. In reality it is God, not we, who initiates the transformation of the world. We are here not to transform but to be transformed, to accept the changes that grace will bring about. God's powerful presence, in the world, for the world, will become the agent of our transformation. We are called, not to manage it all, but to be his instruments, to surrender our gifts of executive skill into God's capable hands.

In her book *The Human Condition*, Hannah Arendt mentions the critical shift in thought and science that took place during the seventeenth century. This change, she says, was more radical than a simple reversal of the established traditional order between contemplation and doing. "Strictly speaking," Arendt says, the reversal concerned "only the relationship between thinking and doing, whereas contemplation, in the original sense of beholding the truth, was altogether eliminated."[1]

Clearly, it is time to re-weave the fabric. One of the lost threads of our Western society is contemplation. Another Hannah, the Hannah of Scripture, is credited with having invented this inward form of prayer. In popular belief, Elkanah's wife, who spent long hours in the Temple with her Lord, experienced prayer in a new way, different from the traditional liturgical prayer of the gathered assembly. Another great figure of Scripture, Miriam, could equally be credited with making praise and rejoicing an everyday affair. Once again it is time to embrace the whole vision Hannah and Miriam knew. The world, even the executive world, is not ours but God's. We help transform the world when we remember God's ways, when we surrender to intimacy with the Power who drives the planets and the stars.

The American philosopher William James was fond of the expression "cash value." In his essay, "The Notion of Truth," he framed the issue of belief: "Grant an idea or belief to be true, what difference will its being true make in anyone's actual life? How will the truth be realized? What experiences will be different from those which would obtain if the belief were false? What, in short, is the truth's cash-value in experiential terms?" Businesspeople and entrepreneurs measure truth by results. In fact, the gospels measure it the same way. But the gospels tell us we will not earn salvation by our activities. To try to earn salvation is delusionary. Instead, our task is to accept wholeness as a gift, and at the same time to accept the reality of things, that God is ruler over the whole enterprise of human effort. This truth, when grasped and assimilated, transforms us. James says further: "Truth *happens* to an idea. It becomes true, it is made true by events. Its verity *is* in fact an event, a process: the process namely of verifying itself, its veri-*fication*."[2] The conclusion we may reach is that as we live God's word it becomes true for ourselves and for others: truth *happens* to us. But how? The answer we need to accept is difficult for those who call themselves people of action. The reality is that truth happens to us through contemplation. In prayer and in consciousness we fix our eyes on God; we regard him, we see him, with our mind's eye. We nourish that vision with scripture, conversation, images, and stories. But most of all we see God in our experience. By reflecting on God's presence in our day-to-day lives, including our business lives, truth dawns on us. We see the Lord as being in charge, one who rules over the enterprise, one who rules in our hearts. Slowly, we begin to live in harmony with truth.

Effectiveness, which is basic to healthy enterprise, calls for a clear and accurate perception of things as they are. This effectiveness is usually seen in terms of management and planning. But what comes before anything else, and makes good management and planning possible, is a whole, unified vision of the world. Effectiveness begins in God; our strength is rooted in Him. *In Him we live and move and have our being* (Acts 17:28 KJV). Our effectiveness is heightened by reflection, by understanding first of all objectives, goals, and resources, by accurately sensing our own starting points from which to exercise authority. When God is seen as master of the marketplace, the scales fall from our eyes. Our vision becomes clear. Seeing the marketplace as God's terrain changes our perception of what we do there. From this understanding a new purpose flows. Now we experience commitment, resolution, singleness of heart. We know where we are going, what we want to build, whose people we are destined to become. We understand at last that God is in charge and that he will guide us into new kinds of understanding. *If Yahweh does not build the house, in vain do the masons toil* (Psalm 127:1).

Many of our idols have fallen. Many empire builders have betrayed our trust, laying up selfish treasures. Because of our disappointment, we who are both executives and believers have become cynical about the entrepreneurial dream. Yet with our disillusionment comes insight. The structures of our lives are not material; they are structures of belief. Belief is the linchpin of business and enterprise. Belief is the factor that sustains Wall Street, the essential investment bankers call confidence. Our countries, our companies, our churches, our civilization, all are resting on a somewhat faulty foundation of trust. Have we given Yahweh credit for his role in sustaining the value of the dollar, the deutsche mark, the yen? Have we fully imagined our corporations, our professional agendas, in the light of God? We need to quicken our belief, to heighten our level of faith. Somehow, in spite of our disenchantment, we need to recover the simplicity and energy of the converted heart. Our great-grandparents, raised in poverty, gifted with far less education and material comfort than we, may serve as examples here. They were the architects of our achievement; they are our inheritance. Did they give us nothing more than a material legacy, a bounty of goods to be used up and tossed away? Following behind us, will there be others, younger than ourselves, who have not taken prosperity for granted? Perhaps they will come to an understanding of faith still deeper than our own. Does the next generation continue to cherish dreams of enterprise and achievement that we no longer hold? Reflection is needed here. When we raise up ideals for generations that follow us, what precisely are we asking others to believe in? Is it ourselves and our own competence we trust? Or is our faith in someone greater than us, a God whose power exceeds our limits of imagination?

Executive work is conceptual. We are executives not because we govern other workers but because we seek goals. We set out in search of a large-scale plan. Whether our objective is the opening of international markets or the development of local franchises, we have some supposed good in view. One company goes under; another opens up. New entrepreneurs are excited as children who want to get in on the game. "I'm starting my own desktop operation." "I've made an investment in computer graphics, working out of my house." "I've started my own housecleaning service, I have eight bonded employees now." Who is the guardian and guide of this large-scale social scheme? Is God even part of the strategy as we conceive it?

Today, our disillusionment with the marketing process we understand so well is tearing at the fabric of our lives. Theodore Levitt, in his book *The Marketing Imagination*, has said: "Each generation everywhere seems to ask for what its predecessors asked only of God. The special condition of present times is that we have all so suddenly been immersed in such an intensively communicative world that we have become intensely conscious of all the squalor, greed, competitiveness, dishonesty, negation, and covetousness that have, in fact, characterized humanity from the beginning."[3] What Levitt is speaking about is a kind of revolution of spiritual expectations. "A rereading of the Old Testament or *The Iliad* quickly reminds us of how much each told us about the awful presence in their times of ignoble traits." Today, Levitt suggests, we find these traits morally unacceptable, instead of tolerating them, as the ancients did, as a fact of life. "It takes a Geiger counter," Levitt informs us, "to find any alleviating traces in either book of any continuing evidence of civic virtue, honor, civility, humanity, self-denial, and decency." In the Bible and *The Iliad,* he says, the virtues appear "mostly as contrasting examples of how things might or ought to be rather than how they were."[4]

Yet many believing practitioners of Western free enterprise think that we are right to expect more from our economic system, even knowing, as we do, the desperately fallen state of humanity. Thomas Johnson, a banker, has mentioned four ways to reflect on the development of a set of standards against which our economic system can be measured. These include: the design for a just distribution of goods; the need for effective means of increasing the aggregate production of goods; the mandate to conserve resources for those not yet born; and the production of human dignity and the opportunity for goodness.[5]

Given objectives such as these, how could we manage without God in the marketplace? There the religious imagination can sustain us as surely as the marketing imagination does. In fact, both can and must become one and the same, flowing from the same real springs of strength, drawing on the same moral and spiritual realities. "By asserting that people don't buy things but buy solutions to problems, the marketing imagination makes an inspired leap from the obvious to the meaningful," Levitt explains.[6] He reminds us that Charles Revson, mastermind of Revlon, is known to have said he was not selling cosmetics but selling hope, that is, marketing to his consumer's inner self-understanding. Along the same lines is the saying attributed to Leo McGinneva, a manufacturer of power drills: "People don't want [to buy] quarter-inch bits. They want quarter-inch holes." Levitt says the marketing imagination brings us to the "simple essence of things."[7] Surely, this is also what the spiritual imagination must do!

"Assuming that the costs of what it sells are reasonably competitive, it remains the burden of the marketing imagination to find ways to attract and hold customers. It usually takes a lot of long and sweaty effort to get things done, and that in itself may take a lot of imagination. But unless the decision as to what to do is appropriate, which is to say, unless it is imaginatively right, nothing can save the enterprise from disaster. Good work in the pursuit of wrong purposes is more damaging than bad work in pursuit of right purposes. In business, the marketing imagination is the central tool for deciding what those purposes are to be." The purpose of business is to serve.

Peter Drucker, a titan of the contemporary marketplace, takes this notion another leap when he says that the task of the marketer is to *create* and keep customers. By "creating a customer"

Drucker does not mean that marketers are to become gods, having the power of life and death over customers. Instead, he is speaking of the marketer's need to imagine fully the customer who will benefit. The marketer must not only imagine the benefit *to* the customer but must also imagine the customer. Drucker wants the marketer to dream a whole vision, with the customer as beneficiary. That fully imagined and fully human exchange will make possible better categories of enterprise, will assemble new audiences and hope to satisfy them. For the sake of the *people served,* goods and services are made to measure, realistically produced and priced to generate repeat business as well as trial. This is the vision that creates new markets and reaches new goals.

From my view from the thirty-seventh floor, I first guessed at the possibility of a kind of entrepreneurial, even a corporate, poetics. In my first years in business I found out how to grasp—in a single insight, I thought—inner meanings, the inward life or soul of something generally considered to be "only" material. In writing about aluminum and its God-given qualities I unknowingly set out on a spiritual adventure. I ran with a raggle-taggle worldly company of television writers and film directors, not all of whom believed in God. By studying, exploring, and *contemplating* the familiar material, we hunted for some inner beauty, wanting to lay meanings bare. We were explorers, discoverers. Focusing intently on aluminum, we wanted to push back the boundaries of film, to stand television on its head. By reflection, by experiment, by thought, by hope, we supposed that, by some breakthrough, we would *say* something that would move everyone.

I remember, as though it were yesterday, going uptown to the Herman Miller showroom to look at the Charles Eames chair. It was a quest! I was in pursuit not of aluminum, but of beauty, the inner truth the designer sees. Then in my mind's ear came the words to voice it all: "What is beauty? A frill? A trim? Or an aspect of texture and form?" There was vision, too, in the director's inner eye. With a burst of excitement he saw the way to shoot the scene: one continuous two-minute pullback, a visual exploration of one surprising aluminum artifact after another. This brief message, like the four or five others we crafted, was essentially contemplative. Reflectivity? Yes, there would be sun caught in the skin of a skyscraper; yes, there would be the sun's corona caught in the aluminum surface of a telescope. Words were used, but only as afterwords. First, we saw the meaning, as surely as if we had been finding the double helix or the formula for relativity. Mind to mind, heart to heart, we thought we had found something ineffable and holy.

To restructure the marketplace according to God's design for us is more than a matter of Bibles on desktops and times set aside for prayer during the business day. Although these signs of spirituality are worthwhile, they are still no more than random leaves of grass cropping up through the cracks of Wall Street. Everywhere in our business lives, psalms, prayers, and inspirational sayings may spring up. They remind us to trust God like lilies of the field and birds of the air. Nonscriptural wisdom sayings also strengthen us. They encourage us to hold on or invite us to reach for high ideals. At the law firm of Monroe and Lemann in New Orleans, these words were part of the company's spirit from early days: "The tendency to persevere—to persist, in spite of difficulties, hardships, and impossibilities—it is this which in all things distinguishes the strong soul from the weak." Cheerful admonishers like Dr. Norman Vincent Peale charge us to rely on God for courage and strength. The spiritual highs we experience in moments of consolation are, however, only momentary roses. The lows of desolation are just as fleeting. What is far more decisive for our business lives, for all of our lives, is a whole, fundamental relationship to the Lord that does not measure itself by feelings. It is a vision that shapes and governs what we think, what we do, what we say. *Whether we live, or whether we die, we are the Lord's* (Romans 14:8 KJV). To understand our right relationship to God is to grasp a principle: a basic law of the marketplace as critical as any theory of money, interest, capital, or inflation.

To say that the aim of business is to serve is to speak not idealistically, but practically. Service is fundamental to the marketplace. Customers have the power to choose; marketers must please, cajole, offer, and persuade. Although no human choices are ever fully free, in a society of abundance marketers find themselves less powerful than they supposed. In spite of all the wit and will in the world, products may be launched, only to run aground. Ideas that seemed brilliant on the drawing board may be rejected by the public outright. Glitziness may be valued by some, yet appear false and foolish to others. Inflated market projections collapse; false ambitions fizzle; short-term marketing plans and long-term strategies fail.

This flawed system, the free market system, with all its vagaries and failings, is what idealists such as Thomas Johnson would push to new limits. We who are people of the promise are feeling a twitch upon the thread, a tug on the rope, the relentless pull of aspiration and grace. Our values are being challenged. Our weary, much-exercised competitive market economy is being called up higher. Johnson would have us, flawed people that we are, do more with and get more from this unwieldy system: produce more, cherish the earth, raise living standards, save lives. Is it possible? Is it within our grasp? Don't structures and systems have their limits? How can we satisfy a whole world's needs? For such an economic challenge, what power can we deploy? Yet we know, with Yahweh's help and with our own God-given powers of creativity that we can stretch elastic structures of belief into new configurations. Estimators we are, but we cannot fully estimate the power of ourselves together with God.

When we exert the power of belief, however, we have a holy obligation. If belief is the ground of our society, the medium by which we develop exchanges of trust, we are obliged to use belief with restraint. We must remember that belief is volatile. When the hydrogen gas inside the balloon bursts into flames, whose lives will be destroyed but our own?

Consider a narrative like the following. In 1985, according to the *Houston Chronicle*, the bond firm of Dillon, Read & Co. earned a share of $1.7 million from a junk bond deal that put the Houston Ship Channel toll bridge near bankruptcy. By late 1992 Dillon Read stood to earn as much as $10.6 million to fix the problem it helped create. The Harris County Commissioners' Court must vote on the proposal, which calls for Harris County to take over the Jesse H. Jones Memorial toll bridge from the Texas Turnpike Authority. The county judge wants a special transportation corporation to study the proposal. If the full plan is approved, the corporation would issue $318 million in bonds and pay the construction firm of Brown & Root to build nine miles of new toll road along East Beltway 8. Some see the plan as a brilliant solution for the financial woes of the bridge, which is heavily laden with junk bond debt. Others question the numbers. They believe the proposal will leave the project worse off than before.[8]

Where is God in all this? One might more readily ask, where are we? We who have grasped on the deepest level that faith is the structure on which our lives depend, we who have come to understand that enterprises must be founded on the rock of trust, we have reason to question the deals that are built on air and sand. Inflated deal making has a long history. This is no twentieth-century invention! Those who abuse the public's capacity to believe are destroying the structural foundations of our own culture. Later, when the buildings sag, when the foundations sink deep into the sand of our self-indulgence, who and what will we call on to shore them up? What power should make the people of Houston trust Dillon Read's "new type of bond that has never been sold anywhere in the world?"

In a letter to the state's bond review board, John Ramming, executive director of the Turnpike Authority, says the Dillon Read proposal is based on "questionable assumptions," "overstated investment yields," and "understated bond interest." Ramming maintains that the projections are unrealistic.

Dillon Read is a respected Wall Street firm. Dillon Read stockholders include Baring Brothers, said to be the world's oldest investment firm—the firm that financed the Louisiana Purchase in 1803. Then, as now, belief was fundamental to long-range plans and large-scale enterprise. Now, as then, if Yahweh does not build the house, they labor in vain that build it. While executives and managers play havoc with the public's power to trust, they put at risk the fundamental faith structure of society, the system itself that we are relying on to bring us through the current economic crisis. Heroes are needed, women and men of valor who will build on the rock of faith, who will play fair, who will lead us out of the wilderness.

Often, when we mention the greedy, selfish behavior of certain political and business interests, we call it pragmatic behavior. This popular usage is a distortion. Another pragmatism—we might call it holy pragmatism—yearns for faith to be lived out in practice. John Loudon, in an essay called "Experiments in Truth," celebrates Gandhi's notion of testing an idea by living it. "Ultimately," Loudon says, "the only validity religious ideas and symbols have is the degree to which they make a difference in our lives. What other reality could they have? Religious traditions deserve respect because they enshrine hard-won wisdom (albeit along with lots of nonsense and cultural baggage). Just because some teaching is traditional does not make it valid in any vital sense, but it makes it worth hearing. The test is in the living." Explaining Gandhi's notion, Loudon continues: "That is, try living as if the teaching is true, and see what sort of person you become, what quality your life takes on." Loudon makes the point that such codes as the Ten Commandments and the Seven Deadly Sins are meant to guide us toward freedom. "The ultimate experiment is discovering how excellence and fulfillment come only in freedom from the drives of selfishness." And he adds, "Performing such experiments in truth requires commitment, attention, and patience. We have to decide to settle for nothing less than the best life; we have to be awake to how and why we do things and what sort of people we are becoming; and we have to realize that living virtuously is a lifelong work of trial and error, forgiveness and rededication."[9]

Loudon's words echo those of C. S. Lewis in his description of the transforming power of choices: "Every time you make a choice you are turning the central part of you, the part of you that chooses, into something a little different from what it was before. And taking your life as a whole, with all your innumerable choices, all your life long you are slowly turning this central thing . . . either into a creature that is in harmony with God, and with other creatures, and with itself, or else into one that is in a state of war. . . . Each of us at each moment is progressing to the one state or the other."[10]

The habits that kill our souls on a larger scale can kill our societies. Self-interestedly pragmatic behavior is part of the problem. But when pragmatism is conceived in Gandhi's terms, as an experiment in truth, it provides at least part of the answer, when the truth that is lived is the love of the living God.

What, then, of those who can't make it in our system? If we who are the shapers and movers of this system are experiencing a crisis of belief, what about them? In the shadows of the fabled skyscrapers, in the canyons, under the bridges, broken men and women who can't or won't take part in our system huddle for warmth, building fires and swigging their pints of alcohol like characters in Charles Dickens. In their faces, too, we of the marketplace come face to face with God. For it is Yahweh, that same Yahweh who shielded us from our youth, who led us forth alive from the battlefield where thousands fell left and right, it is Yahweh who speaks to us in their wantonness. These are the *anawim,* Yahweh's poor. It is God who calls us to account for these people we cannot save, these lost humans whose misery is set before us as we hurry to and from our work every day. Whether we are believing Christians or believing Jews, we are called to practice *tzedakah,* righteousness, justice, holiness. In the faces of those whose lives are blasted, whose bodies are wasted, the Messiah makes himself known. Meanwhile, another voice, the Ebenezer Scrooge in us, mutters, "Are there no prisons? Are there no workhouses?" Conscience haunts us, asking more of us, an ethic compassionate enough to serve our God. *It was You who created my inmost self, who put me together in my mother's womb, for all these mysteries I thank you* (Psalm 139). From the depths of the heart, the words of the psalmist flow, enlightening us and opening us up to justice. We know that the Lord created us to bring his generous reign on earth. Walt Whitman expresses God's presence in the marketplace in these lines:

> *Why should I wish to see God better than*
> *this day?*
> *I see something of God each hour of the*
> *twenty-four, and each moment then,*
> *In the faces of men and women I see God,*
> *and in my own face in the glass;*
> *I find letters from God dropped in the*
> *street,*
> *and every one is signed by God's name,*
> *And I leave them where they are, for I*
> *know that others will*
> *punctually come forever and ever.*[11]

We have only to reach for a corporate poetics: we too will see God in the marketplace, holiness running like fire through stubble in our everyday business lives. Now, in the flush of that knowledge, in the day of our deliverance, we are called to be joyful. Like Miriam on the day of victory, we are ready to shake the tambourine and lead our people in a mighty dance. Yahweh is strong, Yahweh is powerful, Yahweh cares for his people, not one of them will be lost. *Did I not weep for the one whose day was hard? Was not my soul grieved for the poor?* (Job 30:25–26). Blessed are Yahweh's poor; Yahweh's face is glorious in them. Blessed are the people the Lord has called to be his own.

PRACTICUM

1. Try to imagine your life, including your business and personal affairs, as a single, complete whole from which you cannot disengage yourself. Imagine this life as belonging to God. Offer that life to God again, freely, if you can. Imagine God accepting the offer.
2. Choose a Psalm that expresses a wide range of thoughts and feelings that seem to crop up in your attitudes toward God. Go out of your way to read or recite this Psalm in a business setting, or some place, such as Grand Central Station, that symbolizes business to you.
3. Concretely remember your greatest business crisis to date. Be conscious of your sufferings. Join these sufferings to those of the He-

brew people of old, or to contemporary Jews who suffered in World War II. Be grateful for their example of suffering and fidelity.

4. Plunge yourself into a situation that connotes commercial enterprise. Take a fresh look. Specifically look with the eyes of faith. How is God evidenced here? In beauty? In power? Is this scene of enterprise down-at-the-heels? In decline? Is it Godforsaken? Or is God present here within the alienation of this place?
5. Visit an area of the metropolis that is in decline. Mingle (carefully, now) with those who live there. Are they homeless? Destitute? Change places with them in your imagination. What reversals, what catastrophes could have put them into this bad space? Are you also vulnerable in the same way?
6. Pray for a homeless or marginalized individual. Rather than praying for the "needs of those who are homeless"—figure out one homeless or marginalized person you can pray for. Do this for a week. Journal about this or tell your reflections to someone else who understands the spiritual life.
7. When you are making business decisions, consciously reflect on the good outcomes you are looking for. Thank God for the wisdom and skill you have that allows you to

plan strategically and use your resources well.

8. Consciously conduct a given day or week as an "experiment in truth." Keep consciously present in your mind God's measureless love for you and for your executive vision of hope. Live out your values concretely in the choices you make, and gather the light and wisdom gained by a conscious spoken, or more desirably, written reflection.

2

TIME

One of the most significant pressure points in executive life is the shortage of time. Workshops on time management constantly attract us in the belief that if we only knew this or that technique, adopted this or that system or practice, we would become masters of our time. This widespread belief is delusionary. In reality, time is not a problem to be solved. Our perception of time is out of joint. Our approach to time should not be one of mastery. Instead, we ought to treasure time. We should think less of using it and more of appreciating it, knowing its proper value. To think of time as something, unto itself, on its own, an independent, stand-alone factor, is in itself a distortion. Time is neither a solitary cause nor an effect. In reality, time, space, and all other parts of existence are interrelated, interwoven. To see (to reimagine!) everything that is, the earth, the cosmos, existence itself in terms of God changes our understanding of time. *Teach us to count how few days we have and so gain wisdom of heart* (Psalm 90:12–13).

To accept God as the master of time is not entirely a thinking matter. Instead it is a yielding, a surrender to an ancient style of believing. The Japanese philosopher Takeshi Umehara has predicted the collapse of Western society because of our reliance on the philosophical premises of Descartes. The rational liberalism of the West has made the thinking self absolute, exalted man as the master of nature, and recognized only the existence of mind and matter. Umehara says that Western philosophy leaves nonhuman life out of the picture, has lost its relationship to nature and the spirit, and threatens to bring death to the human species as well.

"Is it so hard today to see that modernity, having lost its relationship to nature and the spirit, is nothing more than a philosophy of death?"

Umehara contends that two ancient Japanese principles contribute to the post-modern discussion. The first principle is mutualism, or the ethics of interpersonal responsibility. The second principle is generational responsibility born of the concept of "cyclicity" in time. "This means that human society does not progress, as modernity would have it, or regress. Rather, the same spirit repeats itself in a continual cycle of life, death, and rebirth."

Such a view, Umehara insists, implies a responsibility to all the inhabitants of eternity. It implies, he says, an ethic of being the custodian of the continuity of life instead of being a "one-shot plunderer during man's brief episode of mortal splendor." In the Japanese imagination, he explains, "the other world is present at every moment."[1]

Like many in our own society, this representative of Japanese thought seems unaware of the deep spiritual foundation of Jewish and Christian faith: the omnipotence of God as ruler over the entire universe, the authority that holds being in existence from moment to moment. If we moderns have been false to our ethic and our heritage, our betrayal does not imply that the ethic and the heritage never existed. A deep and ancient wisdom is available to us in our heritage of faith, of Scripture, of worship. If we have failed to practice that faith, our generation can't invalidate what centuries have built up. The vast harmonics of a universe at peace with God resonate in powerful chords in the work of great musicians and artists. The stored treasures of Western civilization can't be dismissed with a wave of cultural rivalry. Rich traditions remain in our consciousness to be found again and followed again, by ourselves and those who come after us.

The word of God is spoken not to a single person but to a whole people, and through them, God's message goes out to all the earth. In the ancient Hebrew myth of creation is an implicit and explicit wisdom of time. Discussing the philosophical ideas of Martin Heidegger, the American philosopher William Barrett puts this plainly. "Man masters beings, but Being—the open region in which both subject and object stand out and are thus not divided—is forgotten."[2] Therefore, these philosophers tell us, nothing is left to us except a will to power over objects. Heidegger confirms Nietzsche's view that this will to power is the culmination of Western metaphysics. The end result is today's world situation in which power reigns supreme.

Barrett, in interpreting Heidegger, is speaking about our Western culture and its pitfalls. One of these is the passion for organization which shows itself pervasively in every aspect of our lives. "The businessman who flies to the country for a weekend, is whisked off to golf, tennis, sailing, entertains his guests successfully, all on a split-second schedule, and at the end of the weekend flies back to the city, but without once having had the occasion or the desire to lose himself walking down a country lane—such a man, we say, is marvelously organized and really knows how to manage things. And, to be sure, he does show an admirable mastery over things; over beings, but not Being, with which he never comes into contact."

Pity the poor executive who isn't willing to lose herself—or himself. To lose oneself walking down a country lane is to take the chance of becoming whole again, regaining the split off part of oneself that needs to be unified and reconciled. To lose oneself, Barrett tells us, is to enter the region of being "where subject and object no longer confront one another in murderous division." Barrett sees this region as the realm of the poet, but thinks it is accessible to businesspeople! "The relation of poet to Being is not the relation of the busy man of power to beings. The latter goes to the country and returns, but without ever really *being* there."

Technological "man" is the final descendant of Cartesian "man," but without the clarity and passion of Descartes' ideas. For Descartes, locked up in his ego, material objects were alien and possibly unknowable. For technological "man" intimacy with objects is unlikely. This person's relationship with things is limited to "knowing what button to push."

Therefore, Barrett argues, "it should be clear by now what Heidegger's final answer to Nietzsche is: it is that Western man has got to fetch Being back from the oblivion into which it has fallen. Man must learn to let Being be, instead of twisting and dislocating it to make it yield up answers to our need for power."[3]

Is it our task to "fetch Being back?" No! Barrett's own phrase is distorted by the very error he wants to condemn. It is not we who must recover Being "back from the oblivion into which it has fallen." On the contrary, it is we who fall into oblivion when we are out of touch with Being. One aspect of this oblivion, this forgetting, this neglect of the truth at the center of our lives, is our attempt to master time.

These words appeared on the front page of the *New York Times*, Friday, September 25, 1992. "JEWISH WOMEN/GIRLS REMEMBER TO LIGHT Shabbat candles 18 minutes before sunset. In NYC 6:28. Outside NYC 1–800-SABBATH. Info 718–774–2060 ADVT." The announcement is common enough on Fridays in New York, signaling the careful Sabbath observance of many metropolitan Jews. But what a universe of meaning is here! In this particularity an awesome secret is hidden: the mystery of space and time. Pinpointed in the concreteness of the Sabbath, all creation is focused in an instant. In this week, in this day, in this minute, in this second, God is, rules, masters. In twenty-four hours, in one revolution of the planet, God's splendor and majesty are honored. Silence, rest, prayer, play, the cultivation of friendship, the pursuit of happiness, all these are tokens of God's sovereignty, celebrations of gift of time. *It is he that has made us, and not we ourselves. We are his people, the sheep of his pasture* (Psalm 100:3).

This same Sabbath-mystery, this peace, is honored by Christians as the Lord's Day, a day of resurrection, a sacred surprise. *If thou turn away thy foot because of the Sabbath, and from pursuing thy business on my holy day; and call the Sabbath a delight, and the holy day of the Lord honorable; and shall honor it, not doing thy wonted ways, nor pursuing thy business, nor speaking thereof"* (Isaiah 58:13 KJV). On this day, in this very moment of time, we will be faithful to the Lord who hallows time. By surrendering to his lordship we will confess that we ourselves are not the masters of time. By lighting candles we will celebrate this wonder.

The Sabbath is a sanctuary in time. Both in Jewish and Christian tradition, there is a rich depth of meaning hidden in this tabernacle for every generation. *For in six days the Lord made heaven and earth, the sea, and all that in them is, and rested the seventh day; therefore the Lord blessed the Sabbath day and hallowed it* (Exodus 20:11 KJV). The meaning of the Sabbath is established in the story of Creation, yet seems to deepen and intensify from one chapter to the next, until it is somehow ratified in God's deliverance of his people in the Exodus story. *And I will make thee to ride upon the high places of the earth; and I will feed thee with the heritage of Jacob thy father;*

For the mouth of the Lord hath spoken it (Isaiah 58:14 KJV).

Even though it is possible to stop working on the Sabbath, it is not so easy to stop thinking. Thought, however, seems to have a more peaceful character when we are not attempting to master space and time but instead to be open to their surprises. With this refreshing frame of mind we imitate, in our small way, the large insight of the thinker Kurt Godel, who is known as the master of the incomplete. "Godel," according to the writer Rudy Rucker, "shared with Einstein a certain mystical turn of thought."[4] Godel, one of the remarkable thinkers of the twentieth century, is a scientist who believed that one *sees* mathematical solutions; that they exist before we find them; that the ultimate goal of all thought and all philosophy is the perception of the Absolute. "When Plato could fully perceive the Good," Godel believed, "his philosophy ended." This is like what was said of Thomas Aquinas, that once he had *seen* God's scheme—in a full mystical insight—his whole life's work seemed to him like straw.

In six days of work and the seventh day of rest a mystery is revealed. Sensitive, with Godel, to the Incomplete, we hesitate to call Sabbathness a perfection. Perfection implies a closed-ended system. Even so, in the seventh day's quiet, a balance seems to be struck, one that evens out the six days of pressure and pursuit. In Sabbath space-time we yield to God's lordship over us. We glimpse eternity within the instant. Through each of the Sabbath's concrete moments, children chasing each other around the sofas, babies clamoring for attention, parents opening the prayer box to say the day's graces, in the visiting, in the laughter, in the news-telling, in the exchange of family visits, in the hand-in-hand stroll through the neighborhood, in the contemplation of the garden, in the praying, in the table fellowship, in all these concrete moments we see God. Sabbath itself is a mystical encounter. It teaches us to tell time. It is eternity caught in a grain of sand or captured in a wildflower. Sabbath is all time focused in a single moment, like the compass that for the five-year-old Einstein became a source of wonder. We hold Sabbath in our cupped hands and see all our history revealed there. When we open our fingers the mystery of existence runs through our hands like water. Yet, though we can't possess it, can't keep the snowflake from melting, even so, time's exquisite delight, the joy of being alive, is made known within the connectedness of space and time.

When our family lived in Kew Gardens, Queens, New York, we once saw a new Torah carried through the streets in procession, reminding us of the ceremonial links with our own Catholic liturgy. Just as it is in Catholic liturgy, the Book is elevated, to be honored by the faithful; as in Catholic liturgy the sanctified bread is carried in procession through the darkened church on the

Christian night of awe, Maundy Thursday, so too is the Torah held high and walked through the town in reverence, and joy by the Jews of this Kew Gardens synagogue. To be a Christian in this neighborhood is to have all the riches of Judaica flung open and revealed. In this generous sharing of reverence, brotherhood and sisterhood take on new meaning, break through boundaries of culture and creed. The Lord is ruler of the Sabbath. It is God who has created time.

From the sacred sevenness of the Christian and Jewish week we draw strength for the management of time. The word *management* is transformed for us; the deeper definition is made plain. To manage is to handle, to cherish, to hold. Into our hands the sacred gift of time is poured by a generous Giver. He asks us to use it well. "Do not squander my gift, for in it all creation is revealed."

Surrendered time is not borrowed, not stolen, but generously given. The time God gives us is truly ours but never stops being his. There is another sense in which our longing to organize is deeply faithful. When we wait upon the Lord, as we do in Sabbath keeping, we celebrate order: the beauty of God's design. Life, our life, is his art form. In whatever corner of existence we occupy, we herald the beauty of God's world. Flowers, dinner tables, music, gardens, gatherings, all these signs of civility bear witness to God. Yahweh is in the midst of us and his people are at peace.

What is the secret of the Sabbath? It seems that observance of the Sabbath requires us to trust God to manage the universe on his own for at least a day. It teaches us how little we trust him. Faithful observance prompts us to trust God more. The effort Sabbath costs us, to let go of our determined effort to control is a clue to our false understanding of ourselves, of the universe and God.

On the day I went to visit the novelist Walker Percy and his wife, that day became Sabbath for me. Though it was a weekday, I remember it as Sabbath time because of my sense of time stopping. An enormous pause suddenly occurred in my life. Jericho's walls came down. As the conversation drifted from lunchtime to midafternoon, I felt the day hesitate, the hands of the clock move inch by inch, the ticking distant, inaudible. We talked about faith, about fiction, about the flowering of belief in Europe in the forties, perhaps some kind of resurrection after the ghastliness of war. But our talk was simple, foolish, funny, easy, not self-consciously intellectual. I was able to become myself, authentic even in the presence of one whose achievement might intimidate me. Laughter loosened the anxiety. "I want to give you a copy of my novel *Lancelot*. I had a few left over. I think you might like it. I usually sell them for a dollar, but I'll give this one to you." In this simple gesture, I saw a lifetime of meaning, an act of belief, of trust.

Eventually I reflected on Percy's spiritual link with Thomas More, the sixteenth-century lawyer who spent Fridays praying. Now and then, I'm told, Walker Percy did likewise. Percy's love of solitude was part of his nature, part of his reflectiveness. Time spent on the bench on the grounds of St. Joseph's Abbey or in the cool inwardness of the Benedictine church, gives witness to Percy's power of letting time flow.

Throughout the mythologies of the world there are many stories about humanity's continuing struggle with God for the mastery of space and time. One story is the Greek legend of Phaeton, the youth who wanted to drive the sun's chariot across the sky. Without authorization, Phaeton seized his opportunity. But as he climbed upward he began to lose his nerve. There were signs in the heavens to indicate that Phaeton was losing his grip. Don't we, in our technological struggle for mastery of the earth and sky, sometimes experience Phaeton's insecurity and fear? In the Hebrew tradition, Adam is the one who oversteps his boundaries, who fails to trust God's wisdom, who loses Paradise. Today, the wisdom of these ancient stories seems profound.

The observance of a day of quiet and rest is God's *shalom*, a celebration of peace and holiness in the midst of turmoil and trial. The world is at war; injustice and violence are everywhere. How can we celebrate peace, when there is no peace? The peace we honor is the peace the world cannot give. Yet this peace that the world does not give, this God-given peace is for the sake of us, for the sake of the world. This we say, not in some never never, but here and now.

Sabbath time surrounds us with loving boundaries. In our celebration of the Lord's peace we know our limits and we are glad of them.

The earth turns again. Now it is no longer Saturday-Sabbath or Sunday–Lord's Day–Sabbath but Monday. Monday is rarely anyone's favorite day. C. S. Lewis said, "The cross comes before the crown, and tomorrow is a Monday morning."[5] Yet in the order of the weekdays there is another kind of blessing. In timekeeping, housekeeping, *economia,* in the order of each day's portion we also experience the grace of time. God graces all days of the week, gives us the grace to make exceptions, to honor him both when we rest and when we work. Also, we can honor him in the reception to the rules: we must work while others are resting and praying. In the grace of the intentional order, we can honor God even when we are the odd-ones-out who work on sacred holidays.

Possibly the greatest pitfall for executives is the longing to be completely in control: of time, of events, of output, of circumstances. Woe to the spiritually minded executive who meant to keep her Sabbath holy, but by some trick of circumstance, could only get her management group together over the weekend! The real gift we make in the Sabbath, or any other day, is ourselves, our own longing for mastery and control. Even in our prayer lives we executives repeat the same patterns; without realizing it, we set up a relentless and demanding structure, one which calls for us to pray five (or fifteen minutes) a day at the same hour. The most difficult trade-off in our business lives is to understand being as doing, to open the clenched fists with which we hold on to time.

Time for reflection is time for excellence. The rushing, the fretting, the constant surveillance of others, the unwillingness to delegate, holding onto the lion's share of the doing for ourselves, while others stand idly by, wondering when their talents will be called into play, all these are signs of time foolishly overscheduled and badly used. The wise time steward simplifies, discards unnecessary tasks, takes clean swipes at the cluttered agenda, and finds fresh space in which to think things through again.

I remember gratefully my first reading of Peter Drucker's chapter "Know Thy Time."[6] His near-biblical turn of phrase was a clue to his own God-centeredness. More importantly, his statement that some things can only be accomplished with large increments of uninterrupted time—this shining insight brought light into my confusion. I had been trying in tiny snatches of time, stolen from unreasonably planned schedules, to do things that were best accomplished with—blessed phrase—a generous margin of time.

Drucker's book was my deliverance, if not from bad planning, at least from bad thinking about how to plan. He helped me to understand—then, and later—that it was my fear of others, the wicked overlords who would not give me freedom to plan my time effectively and well—fear was the demon I had to deal with. Dealing at last with the demons that will not let us plan our time is finally to wrestle with insecurities and fears that enslave us: unreasonable supervisors, unfair schedules, unrelenting clients, unrealistic demands. At last we can come out of the undergrowth and into the clearing, where one can see new options for the use of time.

At the same time we ought to recognize that in the competitive marketplace it is never an advantage merely to "slow down," if slowing down means lagging behind, not caring, procrastinating, refusing to face facts, being unwilling to make decisions. Faith assigns real value to time and does not squander it. Delay is dangerous, for example, when competitive advantage may ride on timely product introductions. In such a case, being there first is no trifle. Without preemptive action, innovations may lose their impact.

To honor time is to revere not only the pauses but also the prophetic moments. Slipping through windows of opportunity, the reflective and intuitive manager has a better chance of being right. Reflection is not denial of time but a way to heighten one's grasp of time. Developing the ability to come to conclusions readily and make decisions with confidence is not a matter either of time-squeezing or of time-collapsing. Intuitive knowledge is rare and visionary. Data-base knowledge is of an entirely different order from the wisdom gained when we make friends with time.

In a paper on "Speed and Strategic Choice: How Managers Accelerate Decision Making," Kathleen M. Eisenhardt of Stanford University offers a picture of the fast-moving decision maker. This person, Eisenhardt's data shows, is intuitive and confident, not because she or he has skimmed the data but instead because many divergent factors, information sources, and business variables have been evaluated, wrestled with, grasped, and internalized. "Anxiety is a major impediment to fast choice," Eisenhardt claims. "Making choices, when information is poor and stakes are high, is paralyzing." On the other hand, she explains, efficacy in stressful situations comes about through "proactive and structuring behavior." Effective decision makers are like chess players, Eisenhardt says, who develop their intuition by repeatedly playing the game. As they do, they learn to process information in patterns or blocks. Because they handle information in blocks, they literally think faster. Real time managers are actually developing their intuition. Intuition lets them leapfrog over traditional, linear ways of thinking, to arrive at fresher, faster solutions. Courageous management and leadership permit quick and highly accurate decision making, with an appreciation of the essential importance of time.[7]

Time pressure is relentless. Time flies, flees, and will not be subject to our rules. Yet, when we enter into a godly understanding, surprising reversals may occur. When we honor time, our own and others', new and loving kinds of cooperation transform our schedules, lift us beyond the narrow confines of conventional time.

In such business phrases as "six months to be a hero" we recognize that business operates by tests of strength and trials by ordeal. We know that each career is judged by time, limited by nonrenewable resources of talent, by unpredictable conditions and circumstances. Time is the precious resource of our lives, the only coin we have to spend.

Possibly the most exquisite time of all is ordinary time. This phrase, used in the liturgical calendar to mean the unfeasted, unspecialized, unremarkable time, points to what is possibly the most remarkable time of all. The basic business of our lives takes place in ordinary time. This day-in-and-day-outness is what real life is made of.

To place ourselves in the presence of God in all our uses of time is essentially to pray in the marketplace, in the same way Jesus did. This connection between God and ourselves in ongoing time, ordinary time, is the real stuff of our existence. This kind of being-present-to-God is prayer, but not prayer of a kind that distracts us from the business at hand. Instead, this kind of attentiveness lets us focus on God in the immediacy of now and respond to his conscious awareness of us.

Recently I acquired a familiar business planning tool known as a Day-Timer, a calendar-organizer that I formerly scorned because I feared to place my creativeness within established boundaries. In the end I came to see the hand of the Lord in this surrender to familiar forms of discipline. In the turning of each page, a full day of grace becomes open to me, and in the discipline of the hours, like the medieval hours of prayer, I feel God's order and a sense of sacredness. To be conscious of God's presence with us in the droplets of time we call experience, what the philosopher Alfred North Whitehead called "actual occasions" is to be graced and set free for unstriving excellence. When we are made free for excellence by a God who forgives and relents, we call others to excel by the way we serve and by the way we shine.

PRACTICUM

1. Deliberately honor your day of rest—whether Sunday or Saturday or Friday—as a specifically religious act. Do not reproach yourself for not having done this before; but

make a fresh start with some particular gesture, like having fresh flowers in the house or listening to music.

2. Play a game with a child. If no child can be found, play a child's game. Let this activity become for you a way of slowing down or letting go of the intense adult responsibilities you feel for the past, the future, and the present. Let God take charge of the universe while you play.
3. Visit the botanical gardens or a nearby nature trail. In your walk, be contemplative. If you don't know how to be contemplative, be what "contemplative" means to you. Avoid making a production of it or sharpening your contemplative style. Instead, be a clumsy, not fully competent, awkward contemplative. Relax and let God do the work.
4. In contemplating flowers, trees, or birds, try to change places imaginatively with the trees, birds, or flowers. Enjoy your role as subject to the King of the Universe. Stretch, expand, unfurl, and experience contentment; be at peace.
5. Visit an older person, or invite that person to visit you. Slow down in order to keep pace with that person's way of life. Allow silences to fall in natural places when they do.
6. Consciously allow stresses to drain away until you feel empty in the good sense of

the word. Try avoiding the electronic, the mechanized, and whatever is high-speed. Walk rather than ride. Read in preference to watching television. Take the time to read the Sunday paper all the way through to the point of total boredom.

7. Write a letter, by hand, or send a card to someone who has not heard from you in a long time and would welcome knowing how you are.
8. Listen to recorded music, classical or modern, but as you would at a concert, without attempting to do something else at the same time. Be fully attentive to the music; let it become for you an experience of God.
9. Read one or more favorite Bible passages aloud, alone or in a group. Don't work at the meanings and interpretations. Just let the experience flow.
10. If you are in the habit of taking office work at home on the weekend, make a deliberate break with this practice for one weekend only. Promise yourself (without making any permanent change) that at the end of the weekend, you will evaluate the differences and consider changing your Sabbath practice long-term.

In all these leisure activities, lean against the impulse to do something, to score, to achieve. Concentrate instead on appreciation, gratitude, praise, and thankfulness for what God has already given to you.

11. In a high-stress agenda, the days often flow together in a mindless stream. Lean against this. Stay in touch with the earth's turning and be conscious of the uniqueness of each day. Get up before dawn and watch the light slowly increase, or deliberately stay in touch with the twilight. Morning and evening prayer are good disciplines here.
12. What would be required, in your relentless business agenda, to leave one day entirely free for God? Follow the example of Thomas More and Walker Percy by creating a day of solitude, a space that is empty for the possibility of grace. Take Walker Percy's metaphor of the human predicament as that of a castaway. Follow out his creative insight that you are the one who can send "a message in the bottle," a message of deliverance and hope. Who are you? What is the Lord asking of you? Is it perhaps merely to accept this sinful world as it is and not as you would have it? Is it possible that you must set a higher value on the distance you have crossed in the sands of existence up to now?

3

CONTRIBUTION

"*What I do is me; for that I came,*"[1] was one of the best things Gerard Manley Hopkins ever said. Hopkins was not only a mystic, not only a supremely gifted poet, but also a fundamental thinker whose contribution stands out over and above the very best of nineteenth- and twentieth-century writing because it creates a new poetics and a new vision. Hopkins was a philosopher who never wrote philosophy. Out of his thoughts came diamonds that cut through cherished presuppositions.

This was a man for whom work was central; his service to God was at the center of it all; yet in his assigned labors as a Jesuit preacher and teacher he never seemed to contribute much. His preaching was laughed at. His teaching was by and large unsuccessful. His poetry lay mostly unpublished in his lifetime. *"Why do sinners' ways prosper? and why must / Disappointment all I endeavor tend?"*[2] Even so Hopkins in a single line of lyric could unleash a whole theology of work, a fundamental understanding of what it means to live for God in the marketplace of thought and ideas. *"What I do is me; for that I came."*

Vocation sings out of this phrase. Each one of us, it says, is called to shine. Wrestling with his own disappointments, calling himself "poor jackself," Hopkins knew all the same that he was to become "immortal diamond." Often, in companies where values have gone haywire, we feel the deep anguish of the brilliance that can't be put to work, talent that fails to find expression. To see one's personal vision for the product, the enterprise, the corporation, neglected, disparaged, misunderstood, and cast aside, this is for each of us a saddening experience, one that threatens to close us up, to burn us out, to block the path of our creativity and energy. Yet as executive and entrepreneur, leader and follower, doer and thinker, I know with the inner assurance of faith that I am called to shine. Hopkins' phrase, "immortal diamond," exposes not just his own brilliance, but the brilliance of every soul in the firmament, the destiny of every soul in the sight of God. Yahweh is the one who calls me to all the brilliance of which I am capable. Even if my organization cannot fully see who I am or what I do, what I am about, nevertheless I am called to be and to do. *"Myself it speaks and spells / Crying what I do is me, for that I came."*

Executives may be mystics, yet express their zeal for contribution in less poetic terms. "To me, the greatest tragedy in life is to be ordinary," says L. MacGregor Phipps, whose intensity, charm, and humor have helped him to manage money and risk effectively through the controversial 1980s in Wall Street, Wilmington, and points west. Characterizing his own business life as a quest, Phipps, who sees business as the life's blood of civilization, describes his eccentric career path. After attending college in Vermont, his way led from securities analyst to hands-on money manager, then to a full year of running a family-owned Minnesota Dairy Queen. Is it hard to conceive of Dairy Queen as a place of meaning and fulfillment? Is it hard to dignify or sanctify a franchise dedicated to soft ice cream?

"This was one of my best experiences," Phipps reflects, explaining how he mastered managerial and customer service skills when he stayed the course with Dairy Queen and "learned how to make the (ice cream) curl." But unlike Don Quixote, Phipps was chasing practical, possible dreams. After fifteen years in the business world, his search for achievement led him to the A. B.

Freeman School of Business at Tulane where he learned to "solve certain business riddles."

"I was the old man in my Tulane class," Phipps remembers. "But, in my years of working I had seen others who knew things I needed to learn." The Freeman MBA plus his Dairy Queen hands-on experience helped Phipps break into Wall Street (E. F. Hutton) on the strength of his personality and drive.

Phipps combined a business degree with his own native audacity to break into Wall Street and become the architect of large-scale programs for Prudential. Carefully calling this phase of his career "intrapreneurial," Phipps speaks of "raising $600 million, using a little over 100 participants." He finds this level of success exciting. "There wasn't a year we didn't double assets under management. Revenues increased tenfold after the first year."

Now at the age of fifty Phipps is planning one more organization, one he can own. His biological clock insists that it is time for him to be entrepreneurial. "So my quest at the moment is the process of putting together my own organization in the financial arena, using my academic training as well as my experience in Wall Street . . . to create some personal equity, to own the company. And I think this may be something that happens after you get so many years of experience. My thought is, if I'm ever going to do this, I better do it now, and if I fail, I emerge yet a wiser man still."

Not power, then, but wisdom, is the object of this executive's reflective search. His quest is not only for achievement but also for the sense of truth and authenticity that comes from having tried. "One almost has to be philosophical. One has to be willing to take a risk. My new organization will build on everything that has gone before. I'm building on the strength and the momentum, and the next chapter will unfold."[3]

Any attentive listener can hear the spiritual resonance in what Phipps has to say. Yet he is not chasing risk merely for its own sake, but for the sense of having gone the distance, having used his abilities to the ultimate. The quest, for him, is everything.

When I drive through the poverty pockets of my native New Orleans, I am conscious of the tremendous failures of society and my own incapacity to change the world. My pilgrimage through these areas of the city is sometimes motivated by professional demands, as, for example, when I am working for the Archbishop's Community Appeal or the program called Food For Families / Food For Seniors. When I visit the troubled sectors of my city I am not slumming; I am not looking down on others, having pity on them, feeling sorry for them—by no means. Instead I am acting as a professional, with the detachment of the professional worker. Like the lay men and women, like the men and women religious who administer special programs here, I look sharp; I look with precision; I am part of an effort to bring more than compassion, to bring practical help and concrete initiatives.

At the same time another voice in me longs for more and is made angry because I am unable to do more. What are the root causes of what I see in these poverty areas? Is a Band-Aid operation sufficient? Aren't deeper and more vigorous actions and better-thought-through solutions in order? This is no place to be melodramatic; this is a place for concrete action, for movement at the policy level. Something significant needs to happen, something that overturns preconceptions, something revolutionary.

Social work, however, is not necessarily the agent of social change. Social work responds to the failures of the economic system and attempts to apply the remedy when there are no jobs or when the jobs that do exist are too demanding for the skill levels available. Human needs are falling through the cracks because the capitalistic system will not, in and of itself, solve every human need.

Can corporate initiative provide the thrust that is necessary for solutions? Is government rather the necessary agent of needed policy shifts? Does entrepreneurism offer the needed energy? Or is an astute combination of all forces—in some kind of uneasy balance—necessary for the transformation of culture and society?

Where can we look for efforts grounded in love? If the love that drives the planets and the stars is a genuine source of meaning and strength, it must also be the ground of every good or even partially good organization. Can we hear the voice of God, however dimly, speak to us through the corporations and enterprises to which we give our allegiance? Are these companies partly good, but riddled with weaknesses and failings? Is the original vision holy, but fading through a lack of authenticity and faith? Is the corporation built on belief? If so, on what belief-system does it rest? Or is the question of God in the corporation somehow absurd, totally laughable, beyond belief?

Stanley Marcus, legendary entrepreneur of the Nieman-Marcus empire, speaks of his life adventure in terms of intangible values. "You can't touch it; it has no smell; it is weightless and invisible, but it manifests itself in very tasteful ways. It is hard to build, but once it is built it has remarkable powers of survival. . . . All of that is by way of describing the nature of a mystique."[4] Marcus relies on Webster's definition of mystique as a "complex of quasi-mystical attitudes" that should never be confused with the ballyhoo created by shallow public relations efforts. For Marcus, mystiques are built on authentic experience, "remembrances of things past, kindness and thoughtfulness, deeds of courage, repeated definitions of leadership and reliability, proofs of devotion to the public welfare as well as to profits, all tied together by the qualities of humor, talent and integrity."[5]

Mystiques, according to Marcus, are not merely staged or invented. Instead, they evolve. "Many who strive for fame get it momentarily, or even permanently, without ever acquiring a mystique. It all has to do with the way the public perceives an individual or an institution, its appraisal of the genuineness and worthiness of the effort."[6]

In the tension between the credo of Gregg Phipps, ascending to the mountaintop in search of wisdom, and Stanley Marcus, descending from the mountaintop with a philosophy of how to be perceived with gratitude, lies a spiritual reality. Business, whether it be retail or wholesale, is built on belief. This natural energy, this aspiration to please oneself and others, to bear witness to creative energies, to make the gift of oneself, to build a reputation, is in great part what business is all about.

"What's in a name?" Shakespeare's question was one that struck home with me in childhood, long before I ever guessed its source. Used in a series of messages from the Ethyl Corporation, the theme "What's in a name?" argued for the importance of corporate reputation. Still another series of midcentury advertisements, sponsored by the Brand Names Foundation, argued that *a brand name is a maker's reputation*. Today, the notion of brand name equity is a commonplace of business school investigations and studies. More importantly, it has equity in the marketplace. Belief in a brand name is a recognition of consistent value, of high standards relentlessly honored, not compromised. A community of faith is forged by the makers of products and their purchasers. This network of loyalty is fragile; it can be, and has been, torn. Noble sentiments and patriotic feelings will not mend it. If the foundations of the marketplace are spiritual, if the rock of our business lives is faith, then we ourselves have nothing more to bring to it than honest skill, commitment, and toil, a new blood, sweat, and tears for the sake of a sagging economy. "A mystique can act like a ghost," Stanley Marcus maintains. "It can come back to haunt you. A customer, disappointed by a defective piece of merchandise or offended by the taste of an advertisement, might very well say, 'I would not have expected anything different from another store, but I feel let down that Nieman-Marcus would be so irresponsible.'"[7]

Not every customer invests so much of himself or herself in a name. Yet there are many of us for whom the experience of shopping in a given store, and expecting a certain level of merchandise and service, is indeed a remembrance of things past, a compact of trust. The names of the great stores that are no longer—Best & Company, B. Altman & Co., D.H. Holmes—become a litany, a memory that haunts and warns us of still further failures that may yet come.

"Nine hundred shoe companies went out of business in the United States last year," says John

Stollenwerk, ceo of Allen-Edmonds Shoe Corporation. "But we weren't one of them."

Located in Port Washington, Wisconsin, on the shores of Lake Michigan, Allen-Edmonds was founded in 1922. As I approached the town on a snowy January day, I could feel the mystique building: weathered faces, worker solidarity, merchants doing business the old-fashioned way, craftsmanship, people bringing more than mere skill to their work but also bringing pride.

It was what I wanted to believe, but was it true? As a casual visitor, I could not judge. But the warm, almost crazy intensity and conviction of Stollenwerk himself was enough to make a believer out of me. From him I learned of his deep belief in the workmanship and quality of the Allen-Edmonds product; of the commitment of his employees; of the solidarity of workers and management; and of the tough competitive spirit of the group. I heard about a work force coming in to help him rebuild a plant completely destroyed by fire. I heard about Stollenwerk himself crashing his way into an international trade show in Japan, from which attempts were made to bar him. I gained, from others, in small increments, the material to put together a picture of an entrepreneurial hero. From the man himself I heard the language of leadership, enthusiasm, anger, Sunday-School morality, a grinning insistence that business ethics is simple and goes back to Cain and Abel and to Adam and Eve. Stollenwerk's anger about much of the hypocrisy and falsehood he sees is a hopeful sign that faith-naïveté has a chance to survive in the American and international marketplace.

After talking with him, I felt that some old-fashioned workplace values have a chance to be rekindled, even fanned into flame. I felt my own enthusiasm stirring again. Some of the weariness and cynicism that is everyone's constant burden now began to loosen, slightly, if for no other reason than the honesty of our talk and my sense that the burden was being shared, not by one strong American entrepreneur, but many more like him.

The principal functions of a manager—planning and directing—are often seen in terms of controlling subordinates. Controlling others is frustrating, demanding, and worst of all, a cause of anxiety, to them as to us. The more we managers focus on how to get subordinates to do it right, the less time we have to plan, to conceive of what needs to be done, to identify objectives both far and near. Time seems to be constantly spent "putting out fires."

One popular book on management style, *The One Minute Manager*, cautioned readers against manipulative behavior. Even so, my supposition is that many who bought the book thought they would find in it a one-minute shortcut to control. Management conceived of as a form of control or manipulation eventually causes trouble. This false and narrow-minded view of the manager's role is often counterproductive. The manager who concentrates on running a department may be missing the point. The manager needs to focus on the vision or the dream that is calling him or her, and, in collaborative settings, bring that vision into focus for colleagues. Such a focus on outward contribution moves beyond the self, seeks a reward that others can appreciate. *No; the greatest among you must behave as if he were the least, the leader as if he were the one who serves* (Luke 22:26,27). Good leaders are good followers.

"We were cursed with vision," says my mother, Helen Dietrich, reflecting on a fifty-year entrepreneurial career and the influence of certain family members as business mentors. Dietrich is the founder of three corporations and more than three business ventures. Her first, a court-reporting venture, gained high standing in the 1940s and 1950s. The second, a tourism company, became the destination management firm that has held center stage in the New Orleans scene throughout the 1970s and 1980s. Concurrent with both of these ventures, she founded a publishing firm and a literary agency that have become well known throughout the region.

Interestingly, Dietrich's early interest was in education and social work. She soon realized she could best help change society by doing what she loved best. One mentor she often mentions is my grandmother, Lucy Russell, who, as a member of the Louisiana State Department of Conservation in the 1920s, founded *The Conservationist,* a magazine dedicated to environmental questions that is still being published in the 1990s.

What was the vision they were "cursed with"? Both women, I think, were animated by a love of city, state, and region. "New Orleans needs this." "Louisiana would benefit from this." For them, building community was a way of being led by the Spirit. I know both of them as Bible people, who read Scripture every day. *Where there is no vision, the people get out of hand; blessed are they who keep the Precept* (Proverbs 29:18).

In 1980 my mother had a close brush with death. After recovering, she said, "What can I do for this business that is uniquely mine, something that wouldn't have happened if I had died, something nobody else can do?"

How many managers understand their call to focus on contribution in this way? How many are asking themselves that toughest of all questions—what can I do for this enterprise (whether or not I own it)—that needs to be done, and that nobody else is able to do? How many managers are fully able to speak from a corporate poetics, to dream a corporate and collective dream?

PRACTICUM

1. Gather a group together from your company or organization and tell the story of the cor-

poration and its purpose in your own terms. Start from your own experience. Who are you? Why did you join this organization? What do you see as the company's reason for being and your reason for being part of it? Reflect on this privately or with others whom you can trust. Is the company's contribution one you can comfortably assent to as a necessary element in a good society? Do you believe in the company and its aims, even if there are things about the corporation that do not satisfy you?

2. Make a list of the ways you have contributed to the good of your company, your fellow executives, or society at large. Have you given God the credit for your achievements and your plans? Have you enjoyed the power and creativity you legitimately exercise in your management role?
3. Make a personal pilgrimage to some part of your organization that symbolizes the heart and soul of the enterprise. Dr. Gary Costley of the Kellogg Company once told me he did this by going to the plant and watching the Cornflakes come off the line. For others, a visit to the corporate park may begin to symbolize what the corporation is all about. Still another pilgrimage may be to the executive boardroom, where portraits of the founders look down from the walls. What is your relationship to these corporate and entre-

preneurial forebears? As inheritors of their vision, do you understand them? Do they baffle you? Do you see yourself as connected to them, and carrying their vision on?

4. Visit (alone or with a group) some part of the city that is in difficulty precisely because it does not enjoy the benefits of middle-class entrepreneurism. In such a neighborhood, become conscious of what is being done there for good: an example might be neighborhood centers in which elderly citizens learn arts and crafts, in which food is distributed to the hungry. How does this environment reflect the values of enterprise? Is it also, as corporations are, built on belief?
5. Consider an unabashedly negative example of entrepreneurism: the drug trade might be one; sexual exploitation in its many forms is another. Are there more subtle examples of these fraudulent values within our own organizations? Have we taken these problems to God, or tried to wrestle with them by ourselves? How can we effectively root these values out of our own lives? Or can we?
6. Consider the possibility that the corporation or enterprise to which we give our lives can become a god for us, seizing the central place in our affections and uprooting God from our hearts. Can we guard against this? What does experience teach us here?

4

BUILDING ON STRENGTH

And indeed, which of you here, intending to build a tower, would not first sit down and work out the cost to see if he had enough to complete it? (Luke 14:28) When Jesus spoke with builders and planners, he assumed that they were competent. He looked to build on their strengths in order to persuade them. More importantly he saw them as whole people, whose weaknesses would be burned away by the transforming power of grace. What organization could not heighten its productivity if we build on the strengths of our managers and colleagues, rather than accentuate their weaknesses? Executives move toward productivity and quality of product precisely to the extent that they are engaged in an entrepreneurial vision, one which captures their sympathies and touches their longings. In short, their spiritual lives, which they might not dare to conceive of, let alone mention, in the context of executive or managerial work, or in the context of blue-collar or white-collar efforts, is, in spite of everything, at the center of it all. Their loyalty and creativity are responses, often relentless, to the managerial appreciation they receive. *And some seed fell in rich soil, and grew and produced its crop a hundredfold* (Luke 8:8). *As for the part in rich soil, this is a people with noble and generous heart who have heard the word and take it to themselves and yield a harvest through their perseverance* (Luke 8:15).

My own long view has something to do with poetics and something to do with the way communities are built via communications. "We ourselves form part of the creative apparatus of God," says the English spiritual writer Evelyn Underhill. "It is this constant correlation between inward and outward that really matters; and this has always been the difficulty for human beings, because there are two natures in us, pulling different ways, and their reconciliation is a long and arduous task."[1] This perception of Underhill's may have some relation to what William James calls "the divided self." To what extent is this notion of the divided self a learned response, or a fundamental reality of our experience?

Suffice it to say that when I first began working on Ivory Soap in 1964, although calling myself a Christian, I still did not understand fully that I was part of God's creative apparatus through my work. To grasp this was a work of reflection; a breakthrough was needed.

Didn't I bring to this work of mine all the longings I felt for personal expression, riches of authentic experience gained in family life, marriage, friendship, falling in love? These were the resources from which I formed the things I wrote, messages I designed for my clients and their products. At the time I began working on Ivory in 1964, I was entering into a long tradition. The firm I worked for, the Compton Advertising Agency, had handled Ivory and several other historic Procter & Gamble brands, for example, Crisco shortening and Tide detergent, for a considerable part of the twentieth century. The agency had been assigned to handle the Ivory and Crisco accounts in the 1920s. Although the Procter & Gamble marketing executives who became my colleagues were known for their hard-nosed, tough-minded business judgments and were rarely sentimental, they knew that Ivory represented a heritage, a common cultural understanding. Ivory's messages were not written carelessly or in an impetuous way. Writers had to embrace the discipline of a strategy statement, one that required mention of Ivory's "historic properties," its purity, mildness, and "Ivory's floating characteristic." Even more elusive, but recognizable, was a certain Ivory character, one that everyone associated with this product understood even though they could not easily define it. Writers who developed these messages read their offerings aloud, then waited for a single word of praise: "It's Ivorylike." Hearing this, the writer knew that he or she had captured Ivory's "uniqueness," in a segment of the business world in which "uniqueness" has been overworked and overvalued. This was high praise. I now think this product's modesty, in a world of inflated and inflatable images, was one of its most engaging characteristics. Ivory, whatever its strengths and weaknesses, nevertheless seemed to have an authenticity. It stood for simple things and for a way of life that was basic, unaffected, and sincere.

My experience before joining Compton had included the high world of fashion copy, as a *Mademoiselle* guest editor; the development of the award-winning Alcoa corporate television campaign "The Qualities of Aluminum"; and a somewhat bizarre tour of duty at Norman, Craig & Kummel, where a zany, new advertising philosophy, that of mnemonic devices, was striving to take hold. From each of these I brought some clue to a philosophy of my own devising, based on understanding mythologies, developing mystiques, and grasping corporate worldviews. In working on

Ivory, Crisco, and Tide, all giants of the American marketplace, I came to understand both the *mystique* and the creation of audiences—communities defined by loyalty and self-understanding. Mention was made, not very kindly, by an observer in *Advertising Age*, of Ivory's tendency to represent the world as inhabited entirely by people who are both nice and wholesome. Years later, when I saw the series done by photographer Edward Steichen for the Kellogg Company, showing fresh-scrubbed young housewives in aprons, with children in their arms, I understood how much the product advertising of the mid-century had helped to define Americans in their own eyes as "good people"—people with warm hearts, healthy feelings, and simple, neighborly ways.

When I reflect on my own experience in the development of product messages, I am conscious that such myths are rarely created *de novo.* They don't spring full grown from the head either of Athena or Zeus. When I worked on Ivory I was adding to a tradition that had been developing over time, in which new layers of meaning are added by each successive generation. It is more than a "thing"—in the sense of pure object—because its humanity becomes visible not only in the messages designed by writers and producers but also by the collective understanding they draw on, through interviews with those who are loyal to the product. During this era I took some satisfaction from the development of Ivory messages representing African-American families.

There was wry humor in the development of Ivory's mystique, I found. I remembered *The New Yorker*'s delight in spoofing the Procter & Gamble Company and its exaggerated reverence for Ivory. One of the magazine's cartoons depicted top management in a severe quandary: "The Day the Cake of Ivory Sank at Procter & Gamble." Another *New Yorker* commentary related to Harley Procter's naming of the brand. Legend has it that the name came to him while he sitting in church. *The New Yorker* responded with a biblical citation: "Therefore God, thy God hath anointed thee above thy fellows." From yet another satirical vantage point, a generation later, on the television show "Saturday Night Live," the spoofing continued, as the "healthy-skinned" Ivory women of the 1970s were made to look wonderfully vacant and absurd, doing those all-American things that Ivory people always seemed to do.

In a daylong workshop by one of America's first motivational researchers, I heard long ago, but never forgot, what might be called the song of the shirt. The subject was a report on washday habits and practices. The conclusions were those any novelist could have arrived at by intuition. We might have come to the point much sooner if we had listened not to Ernest Dichter but to Marcel Proust.

A shirt, we learned, is not merely a shirt, an object that gets dirty, thrown in the laundry basket, twisted, crumpled up, stuffed into in the washer, laundered, pressed and folded, put neatly into the drawer again: far from it. The shirt is someone's shirt. The someone is the reason why for the shirt. Giving, caring, tending, providing, these human concerns are intimately connected with the woven threads of a single piece of wearing apparel.

Soap is not merely soap. This meek, commonplace thing may serve as a gesture of hospitality or welcome, a link with other places and times. Things are not merely things; they are signs of affection, concern, interest, gratitude, and delight. These insights cut broadly across our understanding of products and services.

To the extent that things become the bearers of meaning in our lives—whether they be telephone calls or flowers by wire—advertising messages, when they are well done, help to create a large-scale cultural consciousness. This scheme of values is as diverse as the pluralistic culture it serves. At the same time, these messages celebrate the American experience in a larger contextual way.

They tell us that we deserve a break today, or that the night belongs to them, or that they bring good things to life. And we laugh, we understand, we know. We embrace these things as part and parcel of what America is. We gain a perspective on the brands of coffee and tea, and the breakfast cereals, and the chocolate bars, and the flour and the shortening and the razor blades, and the credit cards and the airlines, and the banks and the insurance companies, and the political candidates, the vast sea of endeavor that is our country, past, present, and future.

Reflecting on all this, surveying the scene, my eye comes to rest at last on a box of breakfast cereal called S. W. Graham, with a girl's face smiling at me. She is a freckle-faced kid with red hair and ears that stick out in an engaging way. She has a silly grin on her face and she is holding a Graham cracker with one bite taken out of it. In front of her is a bowl of Kellogg's S. W. Graham Genuine Graham Shredded Biscuits, and I think I have looked the American dream straight in the eye.

"This fiery Yankee preacher and celebrated nutritionist of the early 1800s led the movement expounding the promise that a simple grain-based diet was important for the well-being of both body and spirit. As famous as his theories were in his time, his most lasting and well-known contribution to the American diet is the wholesome and good-tasting food we've all come to know and love as the Graham cracker. Graham, as a food product, retains all the goodness of the grain including the bran. In addition to being an important ingredient in graham crackers, it has been used in a long list of other wholesome wheat-based foods. Whenever we hear the word 'graham,' most of us still remember fondly the crisp, delicious taste we enjoyed in the graham crackers our mothers gave us. Now you can enjoy all the wholesomeness, good taste and good feelings of graham crackers again in every bowl of S. W. Graham cereal."[2]

It is clear that this package copy is a credo, a corporate statement of belief. It seeks to rouse our memory, to gather us nostalgically into our mother's skirts. It wants to profess the American dream. And I think it does so, perhaps more than the consumer who shakes the cereal into the bowl can know. It is clear to me, as one who has lived in the product development marketplace, that to create and launch such a product is an act of faith. S. W. Graham Cereal was indeed a mere supermarket folly, a product that lasted on the competitive shelves for hardly a year. At the same time it was a leap taken, a gift made in faith—out of the best resourcefulness, imagination, creativity, hard numbers, and understanding of the marketplace (perhaps misguided) but also an understanding of the company and its identity at the deepest level. S. W. Graham is an investment of many millions of dollars by a company that doesn't like to make mistakes; an investment by a company that wants to say, "This is what we believe in, this is what we value, this is the benefit we know how to give." So for me S. W. Graham cereal becomes a window on the company's idealism and profit motive intertwined. The box I am looking at is not only shredded biscuits but also an expression of hope in the future. Whether it flies or whether it fails, it has made its statement; it has done its work. With it comes an expression of a simple, even naïve view, that if you put a good product on the assembly line, one that speaks to the appetite and the tastes and the hearts and the health of people, it will be embraced, it will be accepted, it will be believed. By naming it for a dreamer like S. W. Graham the manufacturers declare that they are reaching for more than a profit; they are articulating a dream.

The dream and the profit and the humanity are interconnected. As space and time cannot be divorced except by an act of artificial logic, so the humanity of the people who make the product and the humanity of those who market it and those who buy and use it—all that is a common understanding, a common way of looking and sensing, community in a broad sense, but community nevertheless.

And in this it is possible to see fidelity to a call. On a smaller scale, a family-owned furniture store in New Orleans, Louisiana, celebrating its sixty-fourth anniversary some years ago, offered the following television message to its customers.

Each morning, back in 1914
Morris Kirschman carefully selected
household wares
and packed them into a modest wagon

which he drove through the streets of New Orleans.
His route was rather haphazard.
His items, mostly one of a kind.
There was no broad selection of colors and styles
that's generally taken for granted today.
However, he carried with him one single but important idea.
He knew that if he gave people a bargain, even if he had to work longer and harder to earn his dollar, his customers would always come back.
Over the years, the humble wagon has evolved into a large, highly successful furniture business, carefully guided by Morris Kirschman's son and grandsons.
This week, they're celebrating a 64th anniversary.
And like their founder, they continue to offer you a bargain.
In fact, many. You see, only the wagon has changed. Kirschman's customers are still getting more for their money.[3]

Is this commercial statement of a company's business philosophy and personal marketing faith too commonplace for us? Is it beneath our notice? On the contrary, it is the core of enterprise, the simple faith of the marketer that has been distorted and cheapened by the fraudulent and the pompous, the wheelers and dealers who thought American enterprise was merely a form of exploitation, no more than a way of laying up treasures on earth. The Kirschman family enterprise took business more seriously than that, as did many dozens of other on-the-level entrepreneurs and believers.

The fundamental faith stuff of business, the structure that held so many together in a collective journey, met the payroll, paid the salaries, put children through school and started new households, kept the tax base healthy, and made it possible to think in terms of philanthropy and community service—not to mention furnishing the living rooms and the hallways and the dens—all these are the commonplace things our lives were built on and they are all at risk, precisely because they are the vulnerable and fragile, but collective and valuable, stuff of faith.

Is it wrong to depict such secular things—soap, detergent, cereal—as having something to do with spirituality? Is it wrong, as I heard one critic say, for McDonald's to "create a spirituality of the hamburger?" On the contrary, to see hamburgers and the people who buy and sell them as God's people is to force deeply felt questions into the open. Are McDonald's hamburgers inauthentic? Are McDonald's values inauthentic? Are McDonald's profits excessive? Are McDonald's employees being exploited, or exploiting others?

Such questions, if they are asked at all, are best asked and answered in the context of a whole vision of society—under God, driven by faith, animated by spirit, transformed by holiness.

For those who conceive of, manufacture, and market the products of the contemporary marketplace, these products represent fidelity to an insight and a vision that are the best you have, the best you can bring, the best you know how to do with the talents God gave you, along with the know-how, the vigor, the good competitive spirit, and the drive to win. In all these things the jagged line dividing the sacred and the secular must be erased for the picture to become whole and possibly even clear. Nothing we do is merely material; the spirit of God is accessible to us in all of life. And the possibility of failure, of sin or deception, the breaking off of our dialogue with God, also will dog our footsteps every step of the way. The spirit of God that drives creation drives also these modest forms of creative enterprise as well. To understand this is to understand more fully our continuing human predicament and also the possibility of grace.

To believe in enterprise, to begin again to believe as freshly as we once did, in spite of the failures and the losses and the things gone haywire, this is also part of America's need for faith, and our need to give way to, even to celebrate, the yearning; and to return, by means of what the philosopher Paul Ricoeur calls a *second naïveté,* to the fundamentals of an honorable dream.

In her book *When Giants Learn to Dance: Mastering the Challenge of Strategy, Management, and Careers in the 1990's,* Rosabeth Moss Kanter shows herself to be strongly metaphorical as a thinker. She also engages us, on her own terms and with her own vocabulary, in this same hope for enterprise as the source of corporate and national, even international, renewal. "In studying and helping businesspeople with their professional balancing act," Kanter writes, "I hope also to help America. The fate of America lies in the success of its businesses. As one of the most fundamental social institutions, business impacts on the lives of most of us."[4]

Kanter speaks not merely with businesslike detachment but with enthusiasm. "The spread of the entrepreneurial spirit, through new business start-ups and the revitalization of established corporations, affects millions of people in a positive way, providing new opportunities for them to contribute, to be rewarded for those contributions, and to increase their stock of 'human capital'—the value of their skills—as a result."[5]

I had hardly dared to expect that Kanter would speak in such simple, rousing language, but she does: "Cheering for American companies in the international marketplace," she writes, "is not just a matter of national pride; it is the best hope we have for ensuring that our standard of living can be maintained, let alone improved, for ourselves and our children."[6]

But her concern is not only for maintenance of high living standards for the few, but rather for strengthening the fabric of society at large. "And the social generosity Americans are coming to expect from businesses in the wake of disenchantment with big government—from spearheading charitable fund-raising to forming partnerships with school systems to encouraging employees to volunteer for community service—rests on a foundation of healthy businesses."[7]

The Jesuit philosopher Bernard Lonergan examined in some detail, in his masterwork *Insight* and elsewhere, an ancient world-vision: *cosmopolis*.[8] In reflecting on what Lonergan says about cosmopolis, it seems to me that he calls up a vision of goodness, seen by a people on the way; a consciousness perceived as a city afar off, neither Battle Creek nor Tokyo, but a Jerusalem that is not yet. Cosmopolis is a consciousness rising within us and binding us together in hope, a consciousness that governs not by force but by insight and persuasion. "Cosmopolis is an x, an unknown," Lonergan says.

To tell us what cosmopolis is, Lonergan tells us first what it is not. "It is not a group denouncing other groups. It is not a superstate ruling states. It is not an organization. It is a withdrawal from practicality to save practicality . . . a dimension of consciousness . . . a heightened grasp of historical origins . . . a discovery of historical responsibilities. . . . It stands on a basic analysis of the compound-in-tension that is [woman and] man. It confronts problems of which we are aware. It invites the vast potentialities and pent-up energies of our time [to contribute to the solution of problems by developing] an art and a literature, a theater and a broadcasting, a journalism and a history, a school and a university, a personal depth and a public opinion."[9]

To Lonergan's catalogue of the work of cosmopolis, I would add just one word: *enterprise*. Cosmopolis invites us to dream about how the experience of the Good might be pursued in the practical order among women and men. Lonergan's cosmopolis seems to kindle in me the power to dare. He implies that we can be rekindled by drawing near to the Lord whose power is inexhaustible; the one who is Lord of the Sabbath and also of the other six days of the week; who, when he rested on the Sabbath, did so for the sake of protocol, and not because he was tired.

I say all this because I know the journey ahead is to be made by means of an increasing level of myth and metaphor. By metaphors, whether of cities or city-states, of kingdoms, or of Jerusalems, we will be able to realize the gift of wisdom, of creativity, that the Lord has planted in the middle of our lives:

I came forth from the mouth of the Most High
and covered the earth like mist.
I had my tent in the heights,
And my throne in the pillar of cloud.
Alone I encircled the vault of the sky,
and I walked over the bottom of the deeps.
Over the waves of the sea and over the whole earth,
Over all peoples I held sway.
Among all these I searched for rest
and I looked to see in whose territory I might pitch camp.
Then the creator of all things instructed me,
and he who created me pitched a place for my tent.
He said, "Pitch your tent in Jacob, make Israel your inheritance."
From eternity, in the beginning, he created me,
and for eternity I shall remain.
I ministered before him in the holy tabernacle,
and thus I was established on Zion.
In the beloved city he has given me rest
and in Jerusalem I wield my authority.
I have taken root in a privileged people,
in the Lord's property, in his inheritance.
I am like a vine putting out graceful shoots,
my blossoms bear the fruit of glory and wealth.
(Ecclesiasticus 24:1–30 passim)

Can we experience this Wisdom in our own lives? Can we make this pilgrimage of faith on our own soil? Can we sense the spirit of God in our own tradition, in the creativity and vitality of the marketplace? Can we do so with humor, with laughter, with hope?

Wisdom. The first man never managed to grasp her entirely, nor has the most recent one fully comprehended her (Ecclesiasticus 24).

For those who have lost faith in corporations and institutions that sell goods and market services, one way to go in search of it is, ironically, by leaving the marketplace and living on the mountaintop. One such journey is chronicled in Henri Nouwen's *Genessee Diary*. Another journey, far less temporary, is in Thomas Merton's *Seven Storey Mountain*. Both of these men who wanted the monastic experience show us the life of the monastery as a place that entails both work and prayer, sometimes separated, sometimes intertwined. A monastery is an enterprise, not only because it manufactures jams and jellies, not only because of the casks of Brandy and Benedictine, but rather because the central insight of the founder is to live, pray, and work for God. This vision of life in community is sometimes lost while we are in the midst of it. To revision our own communities as enterprises of faith, entailing work, prayer, and prophecy, we must go apart, be refreshed, and return again to rebuild the lost cities with a new vigor and with the power of fresh grace.

One example of an enterprise dedicated to the transformation of society is Renovare, under the leadership of the writer and teacher Richard Foster. Although Foster would not perhaps describe himself as an entrepreneur, it is clear that he personally is enterprising and innovative. His personal powers of leadership are considerable. He understands how to gather disciples and encourage teamwork. He understands the power of prayer and at the same time the way that spirit works in community. The work of Renovare is faith work. Even so it is of the world, of the marketplace. It seeks to gather resources on behalf of change.

Retreat centers are worth our reflection, because they too are places of exchange. In these remote enclaves, close to the heart of nature and the heart of God, women and men find again the strength they need in a confused world. They are lifted up, on wings like eagles, and dare to dream about world transformation again. Laity Lodge in Leakey, Texas, is one example of a house of prayer dedicated to such a dream. In this place of prayer, believers come and ask God to do a work of grace in them. More often than not, to different degrees and never according to prescribed formulas, God speaks to them there, as he does to me.

Is Laity Lodge an enterprise? I hardly know, but I think the question is worth asking. As with Emerson's better mousetrap, the world beats a pathway to its door. In these two concrete instances of God's work realized among women and men, a model for the transformed organization or corporation can be seen.

When I am supported by the solidarity of a strong league of prayerful friends, when I am encouraged by the monastic surroundings of a place dedicated to prayer, I can remember and forgive the injuries done to me by others, even by corporations.

"You have to forgive persons; you don't have to forgive corporations," a witty believer once told me. He too was wrestling then with the experience of being rejected, unfairly, in a cavalier manner, by a corporation in which he had placed his trust. In his light remark was embedded the not entirely baseless opinion that since corporations exist to protect individuals from their vulnerability as persons, they don't deserve to be loved and forgiven as persons do.

But I have loved, perhaps foolishly, if not a corporation, then at least the way that corporation demanded of me my best efforts, my most creative solutions, my possibilities of excellence. I have loved, too, the network of goods and Good bestowed on the larger community by corporations.

Forgiveness, it now seems, is the work God does in me when I allow him to do it. From the beauty of the mountaintop, in my circle of prayerful friends, where I am loved and supported I can forgive corporations. I can agree to work with them in spite of their flawed humanity; I can return to the darkness of the marketplace.

"Corporations err morally . . . in many ways," says Michael Novak in outlining a theology of the corporation. "They may through their advertising appeal to hedonism and escape, in ways that undercut the restraint and self-discipline required by a responsible democracy. . . . They may incorporate methods of governance that injure dignity, cooperation, inventiveness, and personal development. They may seek their own immediate interests at the expense of the common good. They may become improperly involved in the exercise of political power. They may injure the conscience of their managers or workers. They are capable of the sins of individuals and of grave institutional sins as well.

"Thus, it is a perfectly proper task of all involved within corporations and in society at large to hold them to the highest moral standards, to accuse them when they fail, and to be vigilant about every form of abuse. Corporations are human institutions designed to stimulate economic activism and thus to provide the economic base for a democratic polity committed to high cultural-moral ideals. When they fall short of these purposes, their failure injures all."[10]

Novak did not suggest a mechanism for holding corporations to the highest moral standards. Few of us have the opportunity, as I once did with the chairman of a major corporation, to reflect on the possibility that the corporation might have erred. Far from needing to be forgiven, a company that dared to ask an outsider whether it matched her moral vision restored somewhat my faith in the American dream.

Novak did not speak about the necessity to forgive corporations. This is, perhaps, a little preoccupation of my own. Conscious as I am that the tares and wheat will grow together until the harvest, I have become somewhat discouraged about avenues for rooting out institutional sin wherever it may be found.

Prayer, I now see, is one way out of this deep disenchantment, providing, as it does, the way into a new childhood, a second naïveté. Here, in the kingdom of the blest, the child may confront even the wicked institutions with his or her most confrontational questions. Yahweh has decreed it. Justice and peace shall kiss. New sources of strength will flow to those who forgive corporations and keep faith with Yahweh's vision for world transformation through them.

Samuel Coleridge spoke of poetic faith as "the willing suspension of disbelief." A contemporary poet, Sharon Bryan, has added to this by speaking of a suspension of despair. She advocates this suspension in the midst of failure. Another poet, Thulani Davis, writes of love that takes its metaphor from the infrastructure's decay:

love for you decays
like new york streets
falls short
like heat inspectors
and water supplies
the longer I stay here
the less I even like you
my ceiling gives out
a little each night
and I think of you
little crashes
like birds with bad wings
wake me up
to a certain bitter desire
for radio, credit or car
i could get out of new york
with the proper attitude
you're not that cute
and crying may be good
for the complexion
but so is oatmeal
i'm not that good at it
your love is crooked
running all in my way
leaning, falling
looking for a place to lay
new york is a hard rock
for that sort of thing
people will just turn
and walk away saying

i really don't need this
i was going uptown.[11]

The title of the poem is "Potholes." Its clarity and desolation somehow imply that things have meaning; that someone, someone of power, even if his name is not recognized as Jesus or Yahweh, listens.

PRACTICUM

1. By an act of conscious reflection, recapture in your imagination the dream that you first cherished in your executive life. Write a reminiscence or a journal entry about your first major assignment and its consequences. Did you win an award? Were you singled out for special commendation for the work you did? What was the vision that nourished you? Has it become tarnished since then?
2. Revisit, as a pilgrimage, some scene or workplace that was part of your original vision. Can you, by remembering, reenter that world? Do you remember thoughts you had at the time? Are there regrets? If you are in tension with those memories, can you sort out better now where your own sinfulness was, and that of the organization?

3. Remember—or better yet—visit an important business mentor of yours. What guidance did she or he give you? Write a letter to express your thanks for the development of your vocation that came to you through this person.
4. Reread a book that has formed you as a good manager or executive. Peter Drucker's *The Effective Executive* was a mainstay of my development; another important short work was James Webb Young's *A Technique for Producing Ideas.* Is there an implicit spirituality in this work? Compare the formative influences from these books with other works you have previously read or are now reading which are explicitly spiritual. Can you bridge the gap?
5. Seek out, and consider joining, a group in your city that is considering the importance of reflection in the marketplace. One good example of this is the Crossroads Center for Faith and Work at Old St. Patrick's Church in downtown Chicago. If you're not fortunate enough to find a well-developed group within your community, consider forming one.
6. Pray about the organization or corporation to which you belong. Instead of presuming you know what its strengths and weaknesses are, ask God to reveal them to you. Be conscious of the ways that you are powerless to

change the course of the organization. Pray to understand better your role within the organization and what God may be leading you to through this enterprise, or beyond it.

7. Is there a corporation in your own history that you need to forgive? If forgiveness is difficult for you, outline the things that are in the way of that forgiveness. Consider the ways that forgiveness of the corporation can help you toward healing and wholeness. Explain the situation to someone else, a spiritual friend or director, who can help you to put this kind of hurt or anger into faith perspective.

5

FIRST THINGS FIRST

In one of the decisive battles of World War II, El Alamein, British Lieutenant-General Bernard Law Montgomery told his troops to press ahead. "If you don't make it, the ones behind will."[1] To read these words some fifty years later is to experience a sudden chill, a sense of our own inadequacy to show such courage under fire, a doubt that we, if challenged, could summon up the same bravery.

In the event of another such challenge to our society and its values, would we, bedraggled crew of the latter twentieth century, be able to live by the spirit as these soldiers did? Could we measure up to the example of British and American forces who went ahead, knowing they might fall, but were stirred by the knowledge of a corporate mission, that all would not be lost if others might make it, if some could live to see another day?

Are we now willing to fall, as they did, so that comrades, others, families and—impossible to conceive—posterity, successive generations, civilization, "the world as we know it" might live? This kind of courage and commitment comes by faith not in tangibles but intangibles; the reality of things hoped for, the substance of things not seen.

One of the governing images of business and enterprise over the last few decades has been that of Abraham Maslow's celebrated pyramid of needs. Maslow's thesis is, in brief, that only when the lower instincts are satisfied, will higher impulses make themselves felt and demand satisfaction. Product development is largely based on the view that needs for personal identity, self-satisfaction, fulfillment, and immediate gratification are the governing laws of the marketplace.

Yet a long view of our history suggests that men and women are capable of great generosity under fire and for the good of the whole. Now, perhaps, it is time for believers to construct another pyramid, to envision a structure of primary faith values for the marketplace. Such a hierarchy of first things must be put ahead of second things in order to win through to a greater good: the transformation of society for the Lord, in the Lord, with the Lord.

Os Guinness envisions a hierarchy of biblical first things that would restore integrity and effectiveness to faith in the marketplace.[2] He states them in ascending order:

—One first thing is the biblical ability to persuade: a politics of persuasion is part of the Judeo-Christian legacy; it is what is needed to continually forge a whole people out of scattered and diverse tribal allegiances.
—A still higher first thing is the ability to think seriously and consistently in a way that is shaped by God's truth. Effective engagement with the culture, Guinness says, will not take place so long as believers cultivate an anti-intellectualist turn of mind.
—Still higher, a third first thing is the biblical sense of calling—the drive and dynamism that comes from doing everything in every area of life to the glory of God, in response to a summons from God.

This notion of calling, Guinness says, is part of the dynamic released by the Reformation. Later, he says, it lay behind the rise of the Puritans and the early colonial enterprise. In America, he sees the center of this sense of vocation in work as coming from the Middle West, the American heartland. Guinness maintains, however, that in spite of these Reformation roots, Catholics teach this sense of mission better than Protestants. He is discouraged by the lack of vitality in Protestant understanding of the idea of calling. I wonder if his discouragement is justified. In any event such we/they thinking is surely behind us. Whether its original source of energy comes from the Reformers or from Catholics loyal to the ancient Christian vision, there are many varieties of teaching all with a single message: vocation. *God's gifts and his call are irrevocable* (Romans 29), Paul writes, speaking of the vocation of the Jews. Throughout Scripture we hear that *I have called you by name: you are mine.* The call is not only to each one but also to a whole people, the people of Israel. Is this national sense of vocation a possibility for us? Can we see ourselves as people of scripture, in the same way that the founders of the American society did? In each of the Catholic religious congregations the idea of vocation is seen as leading to a specifically religious call. Catholics today are becoming aware of a calling that comes in baptism, a priesthood of all believers.

Many different spiritualities encourage the same vision. Francis de Sales is known for his encouragement of the lay vocation. Benedict designed a system to integrate work and prayer. Francis of Assisi encouraged detachment of heart within society. Ignatius Loyola offered still another form of the intense experience we call conversion. In the *Spiritual Exercises* of Ignatius Loyola, both men and women are led to offer their lives entirely to God.

Catholics and Protestants alike can rally to Guinness's statement, "Any effective Christian penetration of modern society is inconceivable without a recovering of a deep individual and communal sense of calling."[3] Guinness overlooks an obvious fact, which Christians often lose sight of. Jews, whom God loved first and all along, are called to the transformation of society as deeply as Christians are. The reshaping of modern society will be achieved even more directly when the Jews and Christians live out a common vision rather than a competitive one, when the believing vision of Islam is honored and drawn into the scheme.

—Fourth and highest among the "first things" is an immediate, direct and personal knowledge of God himself. Guinness says that much of what passes for spiritual experience today is little better than a sort of Hallmark card theology, a shallow, sentimental, suburban subjectivism. A spirituality with depth, in contrast, is a spirituality that calls us to the very edges of our understanding, one that, far from making us feel jolly and contented, manifests itself in a drive, an intensity, a discontent with things as they are. Direct knowledge of God moves us to break loose

> from what we have been—to experience a cleansing, a purgation—to be changed, here and now, as well as hereafter, and perhaps most painful of all, to love and to act out of love. Love makes us vulnerable. Love makes us mad, it is what Plato called a divine madness. Most important, love makes us burn for the kingdom—to see the reign of God realized—in our homes, in our corporations, in our relationships. "Knowledge of God," Guinness insists, "is therefore the critical answer" to our current crisis of authority, a weightlessness brought on by the apparent death of God. God's presence, the weight of glory, will ground us in authentic experience, in reality that has the power to transform.[4]

My own life has been radicalized, not once, but more than once, by Peter Drucker's thoughts on putting first things first. In his book *The Effective Executive,* Drucker speaks of those people whose work is constantly scattered by attempts to do too many things, efforts to do many things simultaneously, the inability to say no to diversionary requests. Concentration is at the heart of business achievement, Drucker insists. "Effective executives do first things first and they do one thing at a time."[5]

What if that one thing is to serve God with all my heart and with all my soul and with all my might? And to love my neighbor as myself? With this intention as first priority, the reflective executive concentrates to serve the Lord well in the most critical task that lies ahead. Past and future are equally diversionary. *Now is the appointed time; now is the day of salvation.*

Drucker's first rule for the concentration of executive efforts is to slough off the past that has ceased to be productive. Effective executives must constantly, relentlessly reevaluate work programs to be sure that energy is not being drained off into efforts programs that are no longer productive.

Cutting out programs that no longer work, that do not measure up to today's vision, is freeing. Agendas must be continually pruned; in spirituality, pruning is one of the chief characteristics of our healthy connection with God. We are being pruned, summoned to a higher task. The clumsy, awkward material baggage of past agendas needs to be trimmed away; the interior vision, the sense of godliness in what we are doing, has to put out shoots, attain new growth. Cutting loose from the burdensome past is necessary. Developing a new vision, which on some level entails self-gift, self-sacrifice, and devotion to a larger dream, this is what Yahweh asks of us: to fuse out of our love of neighbor and out of our willingness to try again a cohesive story about our destiny that will lead us strongly into the future.

One of the most articulate philosophers of the future is Wilfrid Desan, who in a large-scale work entitled *Planetary Man* developed a vision of the change in humanity that is necessary to forge a new world. His vision is far from utopian, but rather recognizes the flawed nature of human aspiration and endeavor. Even so, he holds up the possibility of a cosmopolis, a world city and a world citizen. This philosophical statement was published several decades ago; Desan now seems prophetic.

Reflecting philosophically on the nature of goodness, Desan says the saint is the planetary man in the realm of ethics. "This activity can be called saintly when it is noncyclical (its primary motive is not the self) non assertive (its primary motive is not personal survival) and nonaggressive (it does not aim at the destruction of the other). Only when the individual is moving towards the welfare of the commonwealth shall we call him a saint. It is the *direction* of the mobility which counts, for it is from the trajectory that the Observer will know the missile. The absolute of the saint must be the *totum*, and it is an absolute that we shall call *uncontaminated*, since by hypothesis it is not contaminated by selfish motives in its fulfillment."[6]

Desan defines the saint as one who cares for the other in peril without a self-serving motive—or, better said, without a motive that is entirely self-serving. Missionary zeal may be saintly when the desire to proselytize is not completely selfish: "proselytism does not per se exclude sanctity, it may even promote it, and many missionaries have led lives of heroic charity; but it does preclude sanctity when it uses charity as the fundamental diplomacy for conversion without for that reason making the other in peril any happier. The tacit implication, of course, is that the other will only be happy when he is as *we* are. No greater mistake could be made, for it shows a total inability to enter into the angular truth of the other, or even to suspect that there is any angularity different from ours. In being a man of detachment, the saint accepts the plural and the existence of any angular behavior which does not injure the *totum*."[7]

Desan insists that "the saint of our times must not be seen first as a *savior of souls*. . . . Nor must he be seen first and foremost as an ascetic." Only those who are genuinely able to rise above their own self-interest will ultimately command the respect of others. They will be revered as leaders. These are the people whose motives are believed in, who are admired and followed.

"Those who thought only of themselves the night that the Titanic hit the iceberg live in infamy, while the courageous Strausses who gave up their places in the lifeboat are universally admired."[8]

Are ordinary people capable of such sacrificial love? Desan thinks they are. He says that saintliness "hovers over the average man—as a dream, perhaps, but not as an impossible dream."[9]

Desan is speaking not of people in some particular fields of endeavor; not of those in occupations somehow singled out for sacrificial understanding and kindness; not at all. In fact, his very style of thought—the attempt to define humanity as "planetary man"—is predicated upon the notion that each and every individual can and must become a world citizen; that each of us, even though bounded by angularities and singularities, is at the same time capable of living by truth.

What does this kind of holiness look like? In fact, it is difficult to recognize under the heading of religious terminology. The gap in our understanding becomes a chasm when we attempt to conceive of a saintly executive, a transformed manager, a transfigured entrepreneur. New language is needed to overcome the rents and tatters in our understanding. Words such as love and sacrifice seem alien to the marketplace. Yet it is clear that the best entrepreneurial visions are founded in love.

"What I was really attracted to was being in the retail business . . . what I liked was the tremendous variety of tasks . . . I had a friend who was in the coffee business, that gave me the information I needed, the know-how. But beyond being a mentor, she was in the store all the time . . . but I think that sense of her in that place, offering a product which was a shared experience with a friend, that was what attracted me to coffee. I wanted to see people talking to the people they've come with, or maybe the people they haven't come with. I don't think we can document this, but I know there are major social changes going on, including a return to basics, maybe concern about the environment, a number of things that are converging to make neighborhood experiences and simple values very important. I think specialty coffee in the U.S. is part of that. And I think that PJ's is an experience that people can really relate to. That's where our growth is coming from. And that's where I think it will continue to develop in the years ahead."[10]

Phyllis Jordan, founder of PJ's Coffee & Tea Company, a regional franchised enterprise, is only one of thousands of entrepreneurs who design their business lives around the central insight that animates them; the thing they see as making life better for others and yielding at the same time a return to themselves. This basic exchange of the marketplace serves the self; and serves the other. The dream is, moreover, also predicated on a world-vision. Serving in 1992–93 as president of the Specialty Coffee Association of America, Jordan sees the same dynamic at work throughout her field: "The [Specialty Coffee] association brings together people from growing countries and exporters and farmers with roasters and retailers in a trade association in which the focus is the product, and not on which part of the business you're in, and in that way it's a very cooperative effort, one that produces win-win solutions for growers and manufacturers and everybody. We think the organization can only work if everybody along the chain wins."[11]

Words such as these from a regional entrepreneur may have about them a sense of the commonplace, the ordinary. Yet at the same time they exemplify precisely what Desan is speaking about philosophically. "The obligation to strive towards sanctity is the obligation to strive towards the reconstruction of the One and the fulfillment of its urge to be and to survive." To the discerning eye, the creative urge of enterprise is, or can become, a saintly one, when the reflective executive strives to live out his or her inner vision through a sharing of values, not only with co-workers and customers, not only with colleagues and others in industry, but with the world in the largest possible definition or conception of which he or she is capable.

Desan goes further. "Sanctity on the natural level—and no other level is of concern to us—is above all the removal, through atonement, of guilt. Hence it is natural that for our times, bowed down as we are by an immense weight of guilt, the sole means of salvation should be sanctity in action; for therein lies the expiation of the actions centered on self and the return to the oneness of the *totum*.[12]

PRACTICUM

1. Set time aside to make a pilgrimage to some place that represents the kind of sacrificial courage that Montgomery mentions when he says, "If those up front don't make it, the others will." For some, this will entail a visit to a battlefield or cemetery; a war memorial; or the memorial of a significant tragedy such as the Holocaust. What is the meaning for us as executives? Are we building a world in which war can be eradicated? Are we consciously choosing—and are our companies choosing—enlightened paths for the future?
2. Revisit a prophetic moment or work of art that has brought about social consciousness. One example that comes to mind is Rachel Carson's book *The Silent Spring*, which some thirty years ago raised consciousness about environmental concerns. What kind of courage and dedication is necessary to make a life's work that impacts on the level of action? Am I doing this?
3. Investigate an active initiative that is making a difference in your community. For Chicagoans, this might be the National Center for the Laity, a Catholic group, or Business Executives for Economic Justice. How are these (or comparable groups in your own community) taking on large-scale issues with a view to courageous change?

4. Consider the ways that your work as an entrepreneur or within the corporation expresses your personal values. Can you articulate the sources of your personal and professional quest as easily as Phyllis Jordan does? Consider that Jordan's original choice, social work, was unsatisfying, and the same gifts and talents seemed to her to benefit herself and others in the forming of an enterprise. Where do you stand in the life quest? Are you in the midst of a similar shift of consciousness?
5. Make a list of your first things, not necessarily working from Os Guinness's priorities but from your own. Are you living according to these priorities?
6. Review your time record or correspondence for the last thirty days and reflect on the way you have put first things first during that period. Develop fresh ideas on how to manage priorities in the next thirty days.
7. Reflect on the power of persuasion as it impacts in your life. Have you set out to persuade anyone of the merits of a good cause? Have you raised money for a foundation, a charitable group, a church? Have you personally set an initiative in motion that will change the status quo? Are you open to using your persuasive gifts? Are you open to persuasion from others for the sake of the kingdom?

8. Have you taken the possibility of saintliness seriously? Does it strike you as absurd that managers could become saints? Have you reflected on the life of a contemporary person—say, Romero—which has parallels in the lives of great saints in other times? Have you prayed for an increase in your own holiness? Have you considered the possibility that God has a serious large-scale task in mind for you, something for which you are particularly qualified?

6

DECISION MAKING

One of the most critical tools in effective decision making is the use of the imagination, to project into the future the possible consequences of the act. To stimulate the imagination, informed disagreement is needed, as managers with varying viewpoints debate the possibilities and scenarios. Ultimately, however, most major (and even minor) decisions that we undertake in business require a risk, predicated on an informed imagination, but one that does not operate out of full certitude. In no area of business is the act of faith more apparent than in decision making. *Only faith can guarantee the blessings that we hope for, or prove the existence of the realities that at present remain unseen* (Hebrews 11:1)

As the twentieth century draws to a close, the best philosophers and theologians are moving away from a two-worlds scenario. Grace and nature are no longer stacked on top of one another: the line between heaven and earth is not so carefully marked; the experience of grace is a single stream of consciousness. God is present in our moments of experience. Glimpses of heaven are available to us wherever we are, even in the sufferings of the broken world around us.

A practical theology of hope is rooted in the human ability to plan. Planning is our way to envision a perfection that may be somewhat beyond our grasp; planning, even with imperfect resources, helps us reach beyond the disappointments of the here and now.

Planning somehow liberates. As managers, planning gives us freedom to critique our current activities analytically, to come up with fresh and better ways to do things. Planning makes daily decisions easier, helps us to locate trouble spots, and perhaps most important, lets us sketch out large-scale objectives in ways that are motivating to ourselves and to others. Planning provides a framework for encouragement. Planning gives managers the opportunity to lift everyone's sights, to imagine and to dream. Managers who are effective planners will improve their own performance and that of others; heightened enthusiasm often results, with everyone moving toward higher levels of responsibility.

Yet there are dangers, not in planning, but in the expectations we bring to it. If planning is focused on *control*, rather than on *creativity*, planning may in fact be weakening our effectiveness as managers rather than strengthening it. Planning requires that we learn from the past, assess the present, anticipate the future. At the same time the greatest risk in planning is that we will fail through not being open to surprises.

Napier Collyns spoke precisely to this point at the 1992 International Strategic Management Conference, in a workshop called "Developing Scenarios: Linking Strategy to an Uncertain Future." Collyns, a man of thirty years experience in the international oil industry, specializes in corporate planning, public affairs, management training and general administration. Collyns, a member of Global Business Network, wants managers in the oil industry to deal better with global uncertainties. For this reason, he encourages managers to rely on scenario development as opposed to forecasting.

Collyns spends a goodly amount of his time educating managers (and interested publics) in the value of scenarios. This controversial planning tool, which weaves a hypothesis in story form about how the future many unfold, contains all the predetermined elements that the scenario maker can identify. Around these elements, new imagined and projected events, with internally consistent logic, are woven. Key elements in the process that Collyns constantly mentions are the necessity of asking the right questions, the importance of suspending disbelief, and the necessity to move, ultimately, from scenario to strategy.

"I can't emphasize to you enough that in this game questions are more important than answers," says Collyns, whose Cambridge education in the humanities seems to lead him in the direction of a corporate poetics.[1] He uses such phrases as Coleridge's "suspension of disbelief" and argues for the necessity of persuasion as a policy development tool.

During the many years Collyns spent with Shell, he learned that global forecasting of resource availability, pricing, international economic and environmental factors, and all the rest were untrustworthy. But how was one to convince managers, who were long raised on logic and factuality, to move away from forecasting, based on statistics and probabilities, to scenarios that factor in uncertainty as a matter of course?

"One of the things we found in Shell is you had to involve managers at the very early stages. If you don't sit down with them and understand their hopes and fears, you won't be able to influence them. If you think that, where the future is concerned, there's just going to be a continuation of the same, and then it's proved to you that it's going to change, you just have this horrible feeling in the pit of your stomach, and you feel ill for several days. These are very dramatic things, and to be the company that saw it—like Cassandra—was a devastating experience."[2]

Collyns is strongly influenced in his thinking on scenario development by Pierre Wack, who is for him the "fount of all wisdom" in the scenario process. Collyns cites Wack's two articles in the *Harvard Business Review* as definitive. "[Wack] gives many reasons why probability is not the question to ask of your chosen scenarios. One straightforward sentence states, 'The point, I repeat, is not so much to have one scenario that "gets it right" as to have a set of scenarios that illuminates the major forces driving the system, their interrelationship, and the critical uncertainties.' I beg all readers here if they wish seriously to grasp the scenario process as developed within Shell nearly twenty years ago to return to Pierre's articles and not to be ashamed if they read them over and over again before being satisfied that they have seen the light. One nice irony I just noticed in one of Pierre's articles is his reference to a quote from C.W. McMahon of the Bank of England: 'No time is as usefully wasted as that spent guarding against disasters that do not in the event occur.' The irony is that McMahon was sacked this week (March 12, 1991) from the chairmanship of Midlands Bank for failing to guard against disasters which have nearly brought his bank to bankruptcy."[3]

Peter Schwarz, president of the Global Business Network to which Collyns belongs, offers his own viewpoint, in his book *The Art of the Long View,* on the value of scenarios as a guide to intelligent planning for the future.

Three years ago, according to published accounts, top managers at Royal Dutch/Shell Group came up with two scenarios on which to base their long-term planning. In one, reflecting existing trends, regional conflicts plague the world, environmental problems are attacked piecemeal, and low prices shape energy use. In the other, sustainable development takes hold, international cooperation blossoms to combat environmental damage and global warming, and governments discourage fossil fuel use and promote renewable energy. An account in *Business Week* quoted Peter Hatfield, Shell's coordinator of group planning, who tries to prepare managers in 100 countries for any eventuality. "We want to make sure that the decisions our businesses make can exist in both worlds to the greatest degree possible."[4]

Shell is mentioned as one of a growing minority of companies that are forming task forces, mounting experiments, or revising their planning based on the idea of balancing growth and the environment. "The most innovative thinking on sustainable development is evolving in the business community,"[5] is the view attributed to John Elkington, director of Sustainability Ltd., a London consulting firm. Braden R. Allenby, senior environmental attorney for American Telephone & Telegraph Co., sees leaders edging toward an "approach to management that drives a different set of design and cost considerations."[6]

The most important element in all this is the necessity of persuasion. Belief is the engine that drives policy; faith is expressed in openness to surprises from the future course of events. It is striking for one who knows poetic theory to hear Napier Collyns speak of the necessity of encouraging managers to suspend disbelief. What is even more striking, for one who understands persuasive communications, is the importance that Collyns attaches to naming.

In the development of scenarios, belief is fundamental. A scenario must be argued and advocated by those who believe in it; in turn, the creative naming of the scenario makes it possible for it to become known, believed in, and ultimately influential. Collyns has learned in thirty years as a planner that managers tend to cling to their prior belief systems. Effective persuasion, even a risk-taking leap of faith, is needed to dislodge them from unrealistic assumptions, to alert them to the dangers of complacent, antiquated worldviews.

The pressures of any real-world agenda by definition pull us toward the future, creating a distortion and dislocation in our understanding of both present and past. Because of accelerating technology, because of the constantly shifting global agenda, the future constantly appears to discredit past and present ways of doing things. Our lives, as lived up to now, may lose focus and come to seem in our own eyes to lack purpose. These discontinuities appear to weaken us.

Collyns is a good example of the storyteller in action, who knows how to interpret countless small, seemingly fragmented occurrences, weaving not one, but many plausible stories of the future. His grasp of poetic openness to change will help many to bring order out of apparently chaotic experience.

A tie-beam bonded into a building / will not be dislodged by an earthquake; / so, too, a heart resolved after due reflection/will not flinch at the critical moment (Ecclesiasticus 22: 16–18).

PRACTICUM

1. Consider increasing the amount of time you spend each month on planning. Recognize that the time spent planning can become time spent in a dialogue with God.
2. Make a change in the way you plan. Try brainstorming with a committee, a group of colleagues, or an outside consultant the aims you see in your business life and the ways you will be reaching them.
3. Chart the future visually. Experiment with techniques of future charting. Be contempla-

tive in the development of this vision. Be open to surprises.

4. Like Peter Schwartz, author of *The Art of the Long View,* make frequent visits to bookstores. Subscribe to a book review that keeps you aware of surprising and imaginative developments in your field. Listen for the voice of God in these new developments.
5. Lean into technology. Without becoming a "techie" you can still embrace the future with joy when you accept new technologies as a gift to your understanding. Be a Renaissance person! Rejoice in the opening up of uncharted seas in your experience.
6. Consider plunging into a completely foreign culture. Try out Chinese and Japanese cultural experiences; look forward to the pluralizing of America; remember that our cultural heritage is strong because of the diversity we encompass. Be grateful for the changes you have witnessed in your lifetime.
7. Pray for the world; pray to be open to the future; use each day; remember each day as the day the Lord has made.

7

WEIGHING FAILURE AND SUCCESS

The severest temptation in business has to do with the issue of success. While every enterprise is focused on success, false dreams of success and the false display of success are troublemakers, corroding the real work at hand. Making false gods of wealth, success, power, and position dims our chances of taking legitimate pleasure in the good work we may do. For many of us, failure is a grace that leads us to a true estimate of God's place in our lives. *Have you forgotten the encouraging text in which you are addressed as sons? . . . For the Lord trains the one that he loves. . . . Suffering is part of your training* (Hebrews 12: 5–7). Failure teaches us never to rest our security in any human organization or enterprise, entirely. Once we have focused clearly on the one ultimate source of security we have, God himself, all other things in our lives become refocused and clarified. *Yahweh, my heritage, my cup, you and you only, hold my lot secure; . . . I keep Yahweh before me always, for with him at my right hand nothing can shake me* (Psalm 16: 5,8).

There is no more encouraging story of business failure than the one told by J. C. Penney. It also illuminates the difference between preaching ethical business principles and the far more decisive commitment of living by faith. Always a man who tried to live by faith in his business ventures, Penney nevertheless suffered some severe financial losses in his fifties and had to build his business all over again. Under the heading "Starting Over at Fifty-six Is Possible," he relates the story in his own words:

"In the early 1930s I was overtaken by almost total financial disaster. It was a period in which many people became caught in large forces. As money had become—I thought—my strength, so, in a circuitous way, had it become my undoing."[1]

Penney describes how, with the enormous growth of his financial interests, he had assuaged his conscience by giving much of his money away.

"The purposes in which I involved myself and my support were in themselves right and good. I could not bear to cut back on any of them. Finally external forces combined to sweep away the bulk of my personal holdings and I came to a complete stop. To lose money is one thing; to have motives questioned is another, and harder to bear."[2]

It was some time before Penney could gain perspective on his mistakes. He rationalized that because the things he wanted money to do were necessary and good, he had done nothing wrong. More and more money had been needed to help others. Penney became blind to the way he was becoming dominated by ideas of handling big sums of money.

"This self-justification was pathetically blind. My reasoning took no account of self-deception, false pride, humility. I had told myself that wealth made a man invincible, invulnerable against attack even of economic forces. I had to learn that I had been attacked first by my own self-esteem, pride and material ambition. Now, through the working of inexorable law—'What shall it profit a man, if he gain the whole world, and lose his own soul?'—I saw everything tangible swept away."[3]

Penney says he felt ashamed at turning to God because there was nothing else left. Yet, like many others who first have to blame others for their own failures, it took time for him to find the grace to admit that he himself was at fault.

Penney had been a wealthy man. He closed up most of his country estate, Whitehaven, let the servants go, and hid away there. He wandered the grounds like a lost soul, "seeing enemies lurking behind every bush." He began to try to use manual therapy, cutting brush, picking up fieldstones, pulling weeds. "How often had I watched my father pull the weeds that marred his beloved bluegrass! I was not following his example of faith in God, yet I hardly gave it a thought." Penney knew that his father would have told him to stop whimpering, to set self-pity aside, to look his own downfall in the face, and recognize how little had been lost except his own vanity and pride.

Penney was grateful then for the natural strength of his hands and for his country ways of working with them. He began to believe that the ability to work with his hands helped him to hold onto his reason. He wrestled with his own shame, his own failure, yet at the same time experiencing the beauty of the trees, the stones, and the birds.

"What I needed was for my spiritual sight to be restored—only how?"[4] From time to time he found that verses from Scripture would come spontaneously to mind. "For thus saith the Lord God . . . in returning and rest shall ye be saved, and in confidence shall be your strength."

Another day, while he was hefting a stone, Penney paused to watch a blue jay fly overhead screeching, and then settle on a nearby pine branch. "The cedars of Lebanon, which he hath planted, where the birds make their nests. . . ." Penney watched the bird use the branch like a trampoline, then take flight in a blue flash of plumage.

But this was no instantaneous conversion. Touched by the beauty of God's world, Penney also felt a constant tragic sense at his own wrong-doing. He continued, in spite of his emotional disabilities, to do speaking engagements, some of them in his own stores, feeling ashamed and humiliated and wondering what credibility his words could possibly have after the financial losses he had sustained.

After a speaking engagement in Battle Creek he consulted a doctor in the sanitarium there. The doctor was concerned about Penney's condition. He decided to hospitalize him and begin giving him sedatives so that he could rest.

"*'There's nowhere for me to turn but to God,'* I had told myself over and over again. Yet what had I done about it? Nothing. I had not prayed. I could not honestly say I had even tried to pray."[5]

Though he knew he wasn't yet willing to admit defeat, Penney began fighting against the three shifts of nurses assigned to care for him and the sedatives being administered to him. Scripture words continued to come to mind, but he didn't know how to accept them: "Be clothed with humility, for God resisteth the proud and giveth grace to the humble. Humble yourselves therefore under the mighty hand of God, casting all your care on him, for He careth for you."

"It is strange, how in the midst of weakness we can be so strong in resisting God's help; how we can cling to the blindness of our own stubborn way."[6]

As he endured this trial, day in and day out, Penney began to become convinced that his life was about to end. He sat down and wrote letters of farewell to his friends. Instead of bargaining with God (or anybody) for his life, he accepted the idea that his life was ending. When he went to sleep he apparently felt he would not wake up again.

Confused and disturbed when he did wake, near dawn, and saw that he was still alive, he dressed and went downstairs, vaguely planning to have breakfast. The dining room doors were not open. He wandered along the corridor, not knowing where. Gradually he became aware of a "thread of music." It was an old familiar childhood hymn.

Penney followed the sound of the music into the chapel, where a service was going on. Gradually he was bathed, enveloped, in the knowledge of God's existence and love.

"In the midst of failure to believe, I was helped back to believing."[7] He says he felt an intolerable weight being lifted. What was this change, in a man who all his life had been a Christian, and had taken his Bible with him wherever he went, reading a passage every night before retiring? How can we call this experience one of conversion?

The deep experience of failure, the total humbling of pride, the absolute necessity of surrender lead us, sometimes, onto the barriers, where a newer and more childlike understanding takes hold. Suffering is never joyful. The loss of an empire, of a child, of a company, of one's good name and reputation, simply hurts. Like wounded animals we can't make sense out of our suffering. We wander. We feel sorrow. We mourn.

Ultimately, we come to understand that the Lord is speaking to us in our suffering. Why does Yahweh speak in this way? What possible reason is there to deal with faithful servants as though they had been sinners all along?

"Penney, do you know what I think?" said Dr. Short. "Your greatest work is yet to come."[8]

Who has known the mind of God, and who has been his counsellor? (Romans 11:34 KJV)

Many people have come to understand that in a great fall one may experience a great grace. But the willingness is all. Addicts and alcoholics have much to say of this remarkable awakening that comes only in and through surrender. But they are not the only ones who can testify to this remarkable experience of depth and mystery and a heightened knowledge of love.

"Such experiences have in one way or another come to many men," Penney wrote.[9] Almost immediately he began to be healed of his emotional stress. He resumed his speaking itinerary and went home to celebrate Christmas within two weeks.

"It began to seem to me that I had never before really lived. I was spiritually and mentally refreshed, ready for positive steps. I approached prayer from an entirely new direction, the means of bringing me into that intimate relationship with God wherein his will can be revealed."[10]

Penney was baptized. He became active in the Layman's Movement. He joined a business prayer group in midtown Manhattan. "The one thing more needed," he writes, "was to learn humbly how to give *myself personally* to God's purposes for my life. Taking my faith seriously I must seek and find his will for the use of the talents I had been endowed with, and the experiences through which I had passed."[11]

Penney did make money again in time, but thought he had learned a hard lesson, that the possession of money could not guarantee invulnerability and that he should put his trust elsewhere. "On the contrary, the job well done, the inward joy of being in service—these are treasures that can never be taken away."[12]

This was a man who had a new depth and a new liveliness of understanding. He spoke of living each day well. "Every day I was to be given, in which to live and to share the discoveries and meanings of hard experience, was to become priceless."[13]

After the publication of my first book, *Turning*, I had many occasions to speak with business executives for whom the word *conversion* was unfamiliar; or for whom the word principally meant a change of denominations. Many of those with whom I talked seemed also to think of prayer as a recitation of set formulas, the doing of specific prayer techniques. In the decade that followed, however, the widespread experience of prayer throughout the United States has brought about significant changes in our religious and spiritual understanding. Though we are unclear about prayer in the marketplace, a great many Americans—indeed, people throughout the Western world—would be willing to call themselves people of prayer.

Consider the case of a business consultant I will call Harry. Soon after reading my books on prayer and conversion, he approached me to discuss what I might have to say to his clients about integrating God or religious faith within their business lives. I was struck with the fact that he wanted the Gospel message boiled down, pure and simple. He wanted the whole story in one sentence, like the rich young man in the Gospel who wanted to know what he must do to inherit eternal life. "What would you say," Harry wanted to know, "is the most important idea or concept in your book?"

I answered without hesitation. "Surrender. The main idea in everything I have written is surrender." Now I think Harry was a bit surprised. It was not the answer he had expected, perhaps not what he wanted to hear. As he thought my answer over for a minute, his face clouding over, he said, "I don't know whether Americans will like that." For a moment I was rather pleased with myself, thinking that his discomfort meant I must have captured the authentic spirit of the Gospel.

C. S. Lewis describes the experience of conversion-surrender by saying it was a humbling, a being brought low like being dragged across a doorway. There was no smell of orchards, no celestial music playing. Instead it was a compact made in silence and without any sense of glory or reward. For me and for many others who have experienced adult conversion it is clear that conversion is a power struggle with God, a struggle that is completely delusionary in some ways because if we thought we had any real bargaining power we were certainly deceiving ourselves.

Is it possible, I found myself wondering after my dialogue with Harry, that for people of the marketplace conversion would need its own vocabulary? Surrender seems to be against the contemporary American grain, at odds with our characteristic urge to take charge, to manage, to strategize, to win.

Archbishop Daniel Pilarczyk, former president of the National Catholic Conference of Bishops, once made an effort to summarize American Catholic attitudes, especially as they often were seen in tension with authoritarian Rome. He mentioned such assumptions as: law is a tool to be used as needed; teachings about behavior can be changed by public pressure and the political process; if you can change one thing, you can change anything; if there is a problem, there must be a solution; what can be done, must be done; more is better; nobody should have to wait for anything; and nobody over there (in Rome) understands me.

Archbishop Pilarzyk was, of course, speaking about internal and sometimes jurisdictional battles within American Catholicism. He may therefore have failed to mention one of the most severely double-edged American assumptions, the faith we place in the importance of success. The drive to succeed, as healthy as it may be in some ways, is also one of our most serious emotional and spiritual pitfalls. Success, once we achieve it, fails to provide us with the deep spiritual satisfactions we yearned for. Once we have reached the mountaintop of personal achievement, the huge acquisition of money and capital, something is still eluding us. Success is a sly and tricky lover that dances ahead of us like a will-o-the-wisp on a country road. But then, just when we've left everything in pursuit of it, success abandons us, leaves us high and dry.

There's something in us that longs for completion, for resolution. Success, in the sense of business achievement, cannot fully satisfy that yearning. As long as success is out there, tantalizing us, we may think it is everything we want. But once it's in our grasp, we come back to reality, sometimes with a deep sense of disenchantment.

Imagine for a moment that you're Annie Dillard, standing at the sink washing lettuce, and someone calls you to say that you've won the Pulitzer Prize, and now you won't have to wash lettuce ever again. If you're Dillard, and your sense of things is spiritual, your only response to such an outrageous statement is laughter; and honest amusement. You know that winning the Pulitzer Prize will not transform you; will not take you out of the human condition. Tomorrow and the next day the lettuce will still be there.

False ideas of redemption are commonplace and pervasive. Truman Capote, the author of a startling nonfiction account of two condemned murderers in death row, recalls that in one of his extensive interviews one of the murderers said to him that he himself had always wanted to write a great book. The murderer was somewhat annoyed that after his great masterwork of killing a group of people, Capote was the one who got to write the book.

In this man's twisted worldview, writing a great book would have been salvation, a life-transforming event. Other false paths we sometimes follow may include painting the great masterpiece, building the great corporation, winning the landmark Supreme Court decision. Yes, these things are worthy in themselves; yet the lure of the false path is treacherous. To do these things will not make gods of us, however much it seems so from a distance. In doing the great tasks of our lives we must beware of false gods who demand our allegiance.

Time and again the success-driven pursuit of achievements, the reach for stardom, is far more fulfilling while the chase is on than when the goal has finally been won. *What does it profit a man if he gain the whole world and lose his own soul?* When we look for fulfillment in fame and success, things turn to ashes in our hands; sometimes it is good that they do. When we come to the end of cocksure overconfidence, when we stop chasing the wind, chasing false brands of salvation, when we are disillusioned, when we are drained, when we are exhausted and afraid, when we have had it with our dreams of success, we then want to know, "Is that all there is?" Such a moment can be the beginning of conversion. That despair, that disillusionment, that sense that nothing adds up, the fear that everything is leading to a dead end, a blank wall, that is the moment of vulnerability when God can speak to us. That moment of desire, that time of weariness and disenchantment, when the dream explodes or vanishes through our fingers, and we are conscious of the deep unfairness of things as they are, that is the time when we cry out for something that doesn't disappoint; someone who won't exploit or misguide us;

someone who won't disillusion or betray us. To speak about success is then to speak about failure. Both success and failure are ways to God, breakthrough moments in our lives when a radical understanding of our need for God, a grasp of our dependence on God, can begin.

In times of failure we are forced to the wall. We are forced to ask what we are living for. Why me? What's happening here? Am I alone? Does anyone care? Why have all my hopes and dreams come to nothing? Where shall I put my trust? What do I really believe in? Is there anyone or anything worth living for, or dying for?

In failure we are stripped of our pride. Everything we were holding onto has failed us, and the humbling is a chance at grace. Sometimes that same humbling can occur when we've experienced some massive success. At breakthrough moments, moments of clarity, we are one with the prodigal son who forgot the lessons of his youth, who forgot what he already knew and had to come crawling home. This collapse of pride, this consciousness of our arrogance, this learning of lessons we already knew, comes not once in our lives but many times; not only in the passage from unbelief to belief, but again, once we are already believers, and must learn again to believe in the things we have forgotten. "We are not converted only once in our lives," Thomas Merton says, "but many times; and this endless series of large and small conversions, inner revolutions, leads to our transformation. . . . "

John Henry Newman puts the same thought differently. "We are ever but beginning; the most perfect Christian is to himself but a beginner, a penitent prodigal, who has squandered God's gifts, and comes to him to be tried over again, not as a son, but as a hired servant."

To begin again as a prodigal, not as a son but as a hired servant, to experience conversion over again, is a process for those of us who are already believers, and still growing, along with others, in the experience of faith. Conversion calls us to act on what we believe, to trust the word we profess, to take the risk of change. Psychologist John McCall says conversion is letting go of what we have, which is safe, secure, and certain, for what we don't yet have, which is unsafe, insecure, and uncertain, on the word of God and other people who love us. In that experience what we surrender first of all is our fear; trusting that what the Gospel asks us to deny is not our real self but our false self. That real self, strengthened and refreshed by love, is able to be generous in new ways, and falls heir to an ancient wisdom. When we rest our identity in God, drawing all our treasure from God's storehouse, looking to God for the future, counting all our other investments as straw, conversion works inwardly, shaping us and reshaping us until we are blazing with it, our hearts burning on the road. Then we can say, with Thomas à

Kempis: "Once you get inside the mind of Jesus, once you get a taste of his burning love, considerations of your own loss and gain will mean nothing to you."

We Americans, we of the Western tradition who care about humanity, we who hope against hope for solutions to world conflicts and for an international sense of community based on human values, how can we settle for less than a deep and powerful spirit of conversion, one that is both personal and communal, of the people and for the people? We in America who are concerned for the poor and the needy, who want to put the greatest ingenuity into the distribution of goods and the development of just and productive economic systems, how can we ask for less than the conversion of the whole people of God?

The sacred writers of Holy Scripture spoke about God's love for Israel as if she were one person, one people. God's love for Israel was both metaphor and reality as surely then as the conversion of America is a truth spoken in metaphor now. When I speak of the conversion of America, I am not speaking in political terms or from the vantage point of any social critique or ideology. Instead, I am speaking of the possibility that within us as a people there exists a conversion that is distinctly ours because it springs from the base of our own values, critiquing and questioning success when it drives us blindly toward empty achievements and false status symbols, driving us to lay up treasures on earth without any sense of solace from the possession of them, running helplessly toward our own destruction in passions that escalate, making war on ourselves and on others in our hearts. I am speaking in American terms because I believe that there exists within us as a people, in our common heritage of values, so much that is honest, energetic, and hopeful: a heritage of tolerance, a love of diversity, a suspicion of big wealth and big government, a healthy cynicism about self-righteousness, a national toughness that questions every bargain. This practical, hard-driving, feisty character is worth something to God and worth something to the world when that American character is willing to abandon pride, take off his or her spurs, climb down from the Silver Screen, and surrender.

I am speaking not only of surrender but of sacrifice. I am thinking of Jeff who resigned from his high-paying sales job because he didn't want to sell soft porn; John who stopped sniffing cocaine though it meant going into treatment; Martha who walked away from drinking because she renewed her relationship with a higher authority; Peter who began spending Sundays giving out communion at old folks' homes; conversion that pours itself out in lived experience, including managerial experience; conversion that shines with integrity and calls others to repentance.

I come back again to Harry the business consultant who explained to me that sometimes his clients complained about having made it. They've built a company, made a little bundle, but they're too young to retire, not interested in hobbies, tired of vacations, empty, longing for more, not knowing what to do. I counseled Harry to share with them a precious clue: the well-worn path to surrender, so well hidden, because the gate is narrow, and few there be that find it. Harry, being in his heart of hearts (though not sure how to admit it) a believer, is willing to assent to the notion that this path offers a direction for the future. Harry is not comfortable with ancient formulas; he has not found a church that really suits him. He is ill at ease with God-talk; still, he believes in God. "I know what you were saying in your books," he explains. "It's between God and you." I smile a little, answering: "It's between God and me and you." Nevertheless, we agree somewhat. We are clear on several points. Except in God, nowhere else is the treasure so precious, the freedom so abundant, the challenge so real, the satisfaction so complete.

PRACTICUM

1. Be conscious of, and grateful for, the ways you have learned from failure. Specifically recall and relive an experience of failure in

your own life and be refreshed and encouraged by it.

2. Name the person who has provided for you the chief example of strength under duress. For J. C. Penney it was his father; for Penney, the experience of a return to faith was akin to that of the prodigal son, coming home to his father's values, begging for forgiveness. Do you have a similar experience of having to overcome arrogance and pride? Remember it; share it with a colleague if you can; appreciate a similar story from another person's experience if possible.
3. Penney was helped by the Bible verses he had committed to memory. Have you used Scripture, stored in memory, as a help in times of difficulty? Do you know some Scriptures by heart? Consider committing Scripture to memory against the day when a psalm may sustain you.
4. Balance walking, gardening, and manual activities against the head work that escalates in executive lives. Seek the outdoors; be sustained by water, wind, earth, and sunlight.

8

LORD OF THE MARKETPLACE

The idea that business and enterprise may be the most likely sources of world transformation has broken over many of us with startling force. Why is this such a radical, shattering idea? Economics has been the driving motive behind wars, revolutions, conquest, colonialism, and every conceivable social structure from the beginning. What is perhaps a novelty is the notion that commerce might make the world better instead of worse, might lift the yoke of oppression and break the bonds, if not of political, then at least of economic enslavement.

For capitalists the missionary role is uncomfortable and unfamiliar. Socialism, for a century, has proclaimed a scheme of salvation, while capitalism's stance has been somewhat defensive and certainly not fully ideological. Events, perhaps, have been more persuasive than ideology. The collapse of the Soviet economic system is not the result of the triumph of our system. The world, turning to us for redemptive action, may be placing false trust in our flawed system and its unwieldy, scattershot competitive methods, which have as their only virtue the fact that they apparently succeed.

This is no time to proclaim the holiness of capitalism. In fact, a far more fruitful approach would be to assess the weaknesses of capitalism, to accept its role of world economic leadership. Capitalism, for one thing, is headless. No Secretariat of Capitalism has been established to issue position papers in its policymaking. Capitalism lacks a systematic theology; capitalism, above all, lacks a radical spirit of conversion.

But we who believe in the needs of the people and in the power of enterprise to develop nations and are willing to be converted—we are not the promulgators of a new capitalist world order. Far from it. Instead, we are a people on the way, using whatever tool or instrument a kindly or demanding Providence might let fall in our path. The experience of the Western developed nations, jointly committed to healthy enterprise, to personal freedom, to collective action and worker solidarity—this experience we can put at the service of society provided we are willing to do so.

This willingness is the beginning of conversion. It is in our willingness to be converted, to bear the burden, to carry the yoke, that we become capable of the transformation our God is asking of us. The willingness is all.

Today's contemplatives live simultaneously in three spheres. First and foremost they live in the wilderness. This wilderness is not a desert painted with rock formations, shifting sands, and wildflowers. Far from it. The wilderness is instead, more than likely, some desolate city landscape, in which the broken bricks of public housing projects are painted with the spray of gunfire; the endlessly drifting corridors of the inner city, corridors peopled by the desolate and the anguished; corridors within skyscrapers where the decision makers move columns of figures into new configurations.

In this wilderness of the heart (which may be constantly present in any moment or condition of circumstances) today's contemplatives see prophets going before them, dressed in strange garb, eating honey and locusts. In some part of themselves they long to experience the prophet's withdrawal from society for the sake of society. The second sphere for today's contemplatives is church, synagogue, or temple. This is not merely an inner church, a church of the heart, but rather a place of spiritual commitment in which one's fidelity to God is somehow proclaimed.

Although it is not possible to stay there, lost in prayer, for all seven days of the week, the liturgical framework, the ritual, is woven into the fabric of contemplative lives. Contemplatives carry prayer with them, perhaps in a hidden way, like the inner shirts the orthodox Jewish children wear, next to the skin, only a bit of the fringe showing through. Such persons have their religious allegiances deeply integrated into the rest of their lives; yet they are not doctrinaire. They do not imagine that it is their duty to make Catholics or Jews or Baptists of everyone they meet. Instead, they build a temple of peace from a hidden blueprint. To do this they often meet in small groups with other like-minded believers. They pray together. They tell the stories that enable them to act, justly and well, or sometimes not so perfectly, in whatever theaters of action are open to them. The third sphere for today's contemplatives is the marketplace in its most literal sense: wherever things are bought and sold, deals are cut, products and ideologies are hung out for sale.

The believer in the marketplace is buffeted by cultural forces that discourage contemplation in at least these five ways: with a language and philosophy of achievement that appears to be godless; by a mentality of sophistication that sees faith as naïve; by those who stereotype prayer as rote performance and lip service; by an "in crowd" prejudice against faith that makes the failures of institutional religion a satisfactory excuse for infidelity to God; by the failure of "successful people" to practice the inner life and their scorn for those who do; and by the lack of good and modest teachers and exemplars in the life of prayer. Serious prayer initiatives in worldly settings are often lacking. These could lead others to experience the transforming social and personal effects of living by the spirit.

The same success-driven mentality that threatens contemplation threatens liturgical prayer as well. To a success-driven culture both kinds of prayer are wasted time. Within this frame of mind, both Eucharist and contemplation suffer from the same exclusionary prejudice. Both kinds of worship are stepchildren in a world that celebrates the philosophy of acquisition and the pursuit of fame. "Whoever dies with the most toys wins" summarizes a kind of empty-hearted credo. But underlying that, and in my view far more responsible for the current malaise, is the relentless scheme of values mentioned in Rudyard Kipling's poem, "If." God or society requires of us, Kipling suggests, that we fill the "unforgiving minute" with sixty seconds' worth of distance run. To satisfy this relentless ideal the reward he offers is that the earth and everything in it will be ours.

Is the church as institution a stranger to this success mentality? Far from it. Power driven, as society is, by time frames, time lines, and relentless goals, the institutional enterprise often loses its balance. In the Office of Religious Education and the Social Apostolate the work load proliferates; stacks of envelopes mount; stuffing, sorting, postage metering builds up in almost geometric progression. There is always more to do tomorrow than could have been conceived of yesterday. Machines and people are subject to burnout; strategies, agendas, even photocopy machines go up in flames. "It's not brain surgery," the younger executives say, trying to detach themselves from the stress that is an everpresent demon in our lives. Here, more than anywhere, is the marketplace where prayer belongs, yet it is sometimes shunted aside as impractical, beside the point. Even the church as institution scorns prayer when it isn't geared to some specific purpose. We are always, in every endeavor, wanting to know what's in it for us and how we can best play the angles toward specific, success-driven goals.

Theologians Bernard Lee and Michael Cowan have examined the traits of small group praying communities, characteristics that form them as church.[1] These are: *koinonia* or community; *diaconia* or service and mission; *kerygma,* rootedness in the Gospel; and *leitourgia* eucharist or giving thanks. Such small Christian communities are springing up, they say, all over the globe.

Leitourgia or liturgy may be one thing when it is formalized in the worship of a large suburban

Gothic church or a downtown Byzantine cathedral. Triumphant music raises our spirits; sometimes it alienates us with a sense that it is all performance, we are present as spectators only. Affluent places of worship with their silver chalices and stained glass celebrate the beauty of God; often, however, they distance us from the intimacy of our own faith-dialogue with the Almighty.

Liturgy at its best celebrates the downs and ups of the life of the community, linking us to the larger life of the church of all believers. When we are cut off from this earth-connected plan of holidays, harvest days, death-of-the-earth in November, resurrection and flowering in March or April, we find it necessary to reinvent the experience of God that comes to us through the turning of the earth and the procession of the year. Judaeo-Christian belief builds on and transcends the folk religions of every culture; out of the technological stream of the contemporary marketplace a cultural understanding is also being forged. In and through this understanding a liturgy must be shaped that expresses the collective vision, the group-consciousness, a shared spirit of belonging to God.

One of the most striking visions of spirituality in the marketplace is found in the writing and the works of Ignatius Loyola, whose *Exercises* continue to provide an opportunity for conversion.

It is a world view and a worldly view. Ignatius Loyola embraces the world, clasps it with a kind of glee, then lets go his hold and lets the planet spin wonderfully free. He clearly sees all of created life as good. Each person chooses goods from God's abundance of opportunities. Each person is called to achieve great good, to put God's energy to work.

Today's opportunities for power, put to use in holy purposes, are greater than anything Ignatius and his band of sixteenth-century dreamers could have imagined. Science, technology, communications, all the arts, the professions, the sciences, all these are gifts of contemporary life; they have, by all means, dark shadows behind them. Today's follower of the Ignatian way knows that more intense preparation than ever is needed to do God's work in the world.

Education, then, becomes a critical need for followers of Christ according to the teachings of Ignatius. Thomas Bausch, a business educator, and dean of business at Marquette University, expresses this passionately.[2] "The cross worn by the truly Ignatian person of today is that more intense and longer preparation is required than ever before in order for a person to be prepared to exercise the power available to man, but always in a specialized manner. Further, if this power is to be exercised for Christ, for good, the intensity of spiritual formation and theological, philosophical, and other aspects of liberal preparation, must be in proportion to professional preparation.

"Ignatian spirituality and vision, however, calls us beyond preparing students for a career, a profession, or discovering knowledge because it is there to discover; it calls us to intense purpose and motivation born of vision and love, a love that must be manifested in action, not words.

"Our work in the Ignatian university must focus on the formation of students fully in love with their God, Christ, and thereby motivated to direct all their power to Christ in the twenty-first century. In particular, they must be motivated to help solve the problems of social, economic, and international justice in our world today. There must be a call to 'solidarity with the poor,' to use the phrase John Paul uses. But as John Paul puts it, 'Nor is solidarity a feeling of vague compassion or shallow distress, at the misfortune of so many people."

Bausch thinks education should be all about specific action for good, involving hard preparatory work. Every graduate of our institution should with Lenin realize, "That in a world of action as contrasted with contemplation, the question always is what is to be done?" When our students leave the hothouse of the university environment, they must be motivated to ask, "What is to be done by me to alleviate the suffering of the poor?"

Bausch expresses the Ignatian way in simple principles:

The decision is good if it leads to greater focus.
God speaks through obligations no one else can meet.
The Spirit speaks first through the what of commitment and secondly through the how of implementation.
God's will calls for patience.
We serve our fellow man through competence, therefore God usually speaks through growing competence.
We are with Christ when we opt for the poor.
We are discerning God's will if we are thinking with the Church.
All things being equal, God speaks to those needs that are more universal.
Indifference usually precedes commitment and enthusiasm.
God's call is to be pilgrim people.

In a briefing paper given during the turbulent year of 1988, Lee Tavis of the University of Notre Dame sought to clarify the situation of developing countries in Africa, Asia, and Latin America, particularly those in the process of rapid industrialization. His aim was to state clearly the issues facing the countries and those facing multinational managers doing business there. In his analysis, Tavis quoted an interpretation by Robert

McNamara: "The word [poverty] itself has become almost incapable of communicating the harshness of the reality. Poverty at the absolute level—which is what literally hundreds of millions of men, women, and most particularly, children are suffering from in these countries—is life at the very margin of physical existence. The absolute poor are extremely deprived human beings struggling to survive in a set of squalid and degraded circumstances almost beyond the power of our sophisticated imaginations and privileged circumstances to conceive."[3]

The number of the poor—hungry, malnourished people—is growing. Tavis estimated that in 1980 as many as 800 million people in Africa, Latin America, and Asia (excluding China) were living in absolute poverty. For most of them, the economic growth of the 1960s and 1970s did not improve their plight. As many as 70 percent of the children in developing countries suffer from malnutrition, and as many as 300 million people suffer from mental or physical retardation as a result of inadequate diets. Even so, there is some slender cause for hope for an improved quality of life among the majority population in low-income countries. China is one instance of such improvement.

An Ignatian view of world transformation could entail conversion of the multinationals; as in former times, when whole countries were converted to faith in large-scale movements of the spirit.

Multinational corporations forge links between these very different countries and among the people within a country. Within developing countries, multinational products flow to those who can't read; through company workers who are often drawn from urban slums or rural poverty; through the purchase of materials, components, and services from local suppliers. Secondary effects such as these may have strong impact.

Communities short on physical and social infrastructure and managerial capability call on the local multinational subsidiaries. Because of their organizational efficiency, along with global product sourcing and marketing structures, strong multinational linkages exist. Human, material, and financial resources flow across these linkages. The impact on host countries is threefold: (1) the local economic impact; (2) the social results of the firm's presence in local communities; and (3) the net effect of the international economic structure to which they belong.

Are the multinationals a field for conversion? Can the world be made better through them? Some positive contributions of these organizations have been documented. Supporters and critics alike think that multinationals enhance local skills. In a study analyzing various sources from capitalist to neo-Marxist, Francis and Manrique found that the diffusion of skills in less-developed societies through the activities of multinational corporations was the one area of agreement.

Do multinationals increase local employment? Not everyone shares this view. The value of technology is still debated. Technology is certainly transferred, but questions remain as to whether the technology transferred fits the needs of the developing countries, whether research and development should be located there, and whether the price for technology is too high.

Bausch seems to believe that the spiritual and moral formation of managers for the multinationals can be achieved at the university level. But he sees three obstacles to that formation in university education: "First, we seldom build a teleological and philosophical foundation for understanding our basic business system. Second, we seldom develop the profession of business as a specific, honorable, and sacred calling. Possibly we never treat business as a profession, much less as a vocation, a calling. Finally, we have yet to fully internationalize our colleges and schools of business."

The manager of the multinational who is to be educated by our business schools, argues Bausch, must be a highly motivated individual capable of visioning the role of businessperson or manager not just as professional service, but as a calling, be it a calling from a higher authority (God) or an inner drive (for instance, Maslow's concept of self-actualization) or both. "In no way is this to imply that individual wealth might not be a result. I am regularly amazed by the simplicity of life-style, drive for accomplishment alone, not wealth, and the great generosity of many corporate executives, business professionals, and entrepreneurs." Bausch adds, "I am especially impressed by the many entrepreneurs I know who almost appear embarrassed by their wealth, for they have had so much fun and such a deep sense of accomplishment in the process of developing that wealth."

Bausch sees his personal commitment and that of Tavis as formed by their presence in universities (organizations) with a deep religious orientation "where the final purpose of life, as we perceive it, is ever before us. One of the promises we make our stakeholders, and one of the themes that enlivens our institutions, is our Catholic character."

Bausch, however, believes that this same sense of formation develops in other educational systems. He sees the English public schools as one such example, where the demand for public service contributed not only to the building of an empire but also to a moral vision for society as a whole. Bausch also praises the sense of noblesse oblige, which he thinks has permeated the best private schools in the United States.

Bausch concludes that the concept of developmental responsibility calls for business schools to develop new conceptual models of the corporation. "As educators, our primary work with undergraduate (business) students must focus on a broad liberalizing experience. More than anything else education is the development of deeply-rooted habits of the mind that lead the person ever more to learn, communicate, operate with a historical perspective, understand complex institutions, strive for a deep self-understanding including a realized and understood sense of one's own values, and above all in the future's complex and changing global society, be vitally interested in other cultures, societies and nations, and able to quickly learn about and understand them."[4]

Clearly, what Bausch advocates goes far beyond what passes for "community" in many organizations today. Skilled writers and conceptual thinkers create themes and slogans that are meant to create a sense of solidarity within organizations. Top managers proclaim them; middle-management executives adopt them; groups within organizations are encouraged to live by them. The goal is bigger, better retailing; bigger, better banking; and bigger, better package goods marketing. But a terrifying San Andreas fault, a thin line of falsity traces the oncoming collapse. Within the organization, believers who trusted in the slogans and creeds of the corporation try to signal to top management that the ship is foundering, that the game is lost. Community must become more than just gathering the troops, telling the stories, and remembering things past. Community must be rooted in values that do not fail, values that go beyond the self-aggrandizement of human leaders.

Well you know, Yahweh, the course of man is not in his control, nor is it in man's power as he goes his way to guide his steps. Correct us, Yahweh, gently, not in your anger or you will reduce us to nothing (Jeremiah 11:23).

Bausch sees undergraduate business education not only as liberal education but as the nurturing of a moral vision. Students must learn to live within the global community in such a way that they can do justice. MBA programs should internationalize courses; they should also develop new environmental courses that focus on international, nonmarket forces and the analysis of inefficient markets. Developmental responsibility calls business educators, Bausch says, to teach management, business leadership, and the profession of business, as more than a source of income but rather as a true vocation or calling.

Bausch is concerned that management educators in the United States are "basking in a complacency born of success, born of the demand for our product. To break out of this complacency we need to direct our work to the preparation of a new type of manager, a manager committed to the focusing of the powers of our system, of the multinational corporation in particular, to the alleviation of poverty in underdeveloped countries. We should think through how we can prepare students for development especially in a sense where developmental responsibility becomes the hard-nosed and professional action so desperately needed in today's world." What sort of education will be required for MBA candidates to identify with the picture of the just-dealing person described by Jeremiah? A blessing on the one who puts trust in Yahweh, with Yahweh for his hope. *He is like a tree by the waterside that thrusts its roots to the stream: when the heat comes it feels no alarm, its foliage stays green; it has no worries in a year of drought, and never ceases to bear fruit* (Jeremiah 17:5).

In the midst of another world revolution, which some may one day call the Revolution of 1989, peoples West and East confronted a sea-change in the world economic order. We can confront it with fear or with faith.

The poet Federico García Lorca, a Basque living in New York City, wrote these words in 1929. "A few days ago I had the pleasure (or the horror) of seeing the stock market collapse . . . it was dreadful. Twelve *billion* dollars were lost! The sight of Wall Street was indescribable. I spent more than seven hours mingling with the crowd when the panic was at its height. I just couldn't leave. Everywhere one looked, there were men shouting and arguing like animals and women crying. . . . The messengers worked so hard running orders that many of them simply collapsed, and no one was able to wake them or get them on their feet. The streets—the terrible canyons between buildings—were filled with hysteria and chaos, and you cannot possibly imagine the sufferings of the crowd."[5]

For decades of the twentieth century, those who are able to remember the panics and depressions of earlier times have assured the others that it can't happen again and it can't happen here. We know the practical effects of fear. We understand the impact of sin in the practical order. We recognize in a new way the spiritual foundations of the marketplace.

The heart is more devious than any other thing / perverse too; who can pierce its secrets? / I, Yahweh, search to the heart, / I probe the loins, / to give each man what his conduct and his business actions deserve (Jeremiah 17:9–11).

How, then, short of real religious faith in a justice that operates at the deepest level, where the secrets of the heart are hidden, will a genuine moral vision arise to shape the next generation of business leaders? What reality will shape managers who are both practical and idealistic; visionaries who have the practical skills and know-how to begin to accomplish through the marketplace, by means of gradual but significant process, the liberation of humanity, bit by bit, from the enslavement of ignorance and want, and from the crippling effects of fear. *Fear,* Jesus told the ruler of a synagogue, *is useless; what is wanted is trust* (see Mark 5:36). To accomplish this liberation, conversion is necessary. Like Ignatius Loyola, people of action must also become people who weep.

In our weeping we will be following Jesus of Nazareth, who wept for his people and longed to guide them on a holy path.

For decades it has been possible for those in Western nations to distance themselves from poverty, to look down from a pinnacle of affluence or comfort at "the poorer nations," to be compassionate toward the poor in our own society and those overseas. Now the crumbling infrastructure is upon us and we are conscious that the whole system upon which we are depending is at risk. Problematic events converge—poor law enforcement, the drug crisis, racketeering, drug dealing, violence in the streets—to help us understand our peril. We who are already weak and frail must learn sacrifice for the sake of those even more helpless than ourselves. This is our cross; and in this suffering we will be transformed.

By his stripes we are healed (Isaiah 53:5). In the task that lies ahead, the stripes of the suffering servant of Isaiah will become ours. The humiliation of our present predicament, these times of suffering, will no doubt be the making of us. The words of Carl von Clausewitz provide us with food for strategic thought:

"Therefore, if hereafter in another place we examine what is to be done after the loss of a great battle, if we bring under review the resources which still remain, even in the most desperate cases, if we should express a belief in the possibility of retrieving all, even in such a case." The great strategist offers some gleam, not of victory, but of strength-beyond-defeat. "Another question is whether through the loss of a great battle, forces are not perhaps roused into existence, which otherwise would never have come to life. This case is conceivable, and it is what actually has occurred with many nations. But to produce this intensified reaction is beyond the province of military wit, which can only take account of it where it might be presumed as a possibility."[6]

Disillusioned and defeated by a vast metropolis in which he could see no Christianity and little hope, the poet García Lorca wrote:

Dawn in New York has
four columns of mire
and a hurricane of black pigeons
splashing in the putrid waters

Dawn in New York groans
on enormous fire escapes
searching between the angles
for spikenards of drafted anguish

Dawn arrives and no one receives it
in his mouth
because morning and hope are
impossible here.[7]

Centuries before, the same intensely erotic Spanish spirit, flowing in the heart of John of the

Cross, cried out instead of the deep mystery of union with God. The poets are keen observers; they see the degradation of the cities, the enslavement of the rich and the poor, and the oppression in human hearts. For us, now, a new poetics is necessary to see in experience how and where we must apply God's power toward creative world transformation.

It is clear that the new economic world order will not roll down like dew from heaven. The operation of free market economics will now and then have its unwanted and unintended side effects. Yet in all these moments of winning and losing, these risings and fallings of the Dow Jones and the irregular heartbeat of the world economy, there are moments of common vision and common hope; of friendship and solidarity. The humanizing, even the divinizing of the marketplace is as never before in world history, a possibility. We, who are the instruments of that national and worldwide conversion, are both the heirs of a great promise and, in the history of consciousness, by far the most privileged generation.

Even so, in the marketplace one does not speak openly and easily of God. The God-talkers are those whose agenda is combative, manipulative, and divisive. Peacemakers and diplomats move deftly and without bombast toward shared visions of belief without invoking God by a particular name in the public square. In recovery groups many are recovering from the deep distortions of

God-concepts and God-pomposity. Emotionally wounded people grope back again toward a healthier understanding of a power that is both loving and personal. Yet even before the name of God is mentioned and perhaps because of that very reticence, deep loves spring up among business colleagues. Rooted communities of hope and understanding sprout without warning, expressing new idealism. Here God is present. At last, in this underground of safety, grace takes hold. We mention God by name. Prayer is central to the enterprise. Exchanges of spirit cut across boundaries of denomination and creed. Mystical friendships begin, drawing us toward a new politics within our organizations and society at large. God flows from heart to heart. Estranged from some business colleagues by the baffling fact of my faith commitment, I can still enter into limited compacts based on common values, professional commitment, and ideals.

The reflective executive is one who walks by faith and thinks by metaphor; who sees in the terror and anxiety of the twentieth century a call to holiness, who understands daily experience as a call to conversion, who lives in dialogue with God, making intercession for others; who throws her own life into the breach when necessary; who manifests a concern for others; who takes into account, in business decisions, the intolerable sound of the word "trade-off" and at the same time the relentless necessity of compromise; who operates within the realm of the practical knowing that with God, all things are possible; who looks long, looks hard, looks prophetically and with vision at the improbable realignments that take place in society daily; who sets aside, to the extent possible, the biases, the *scotosis*, the distortions of ancient enmities and strife; and who longs for reconciliation, solidarity, sisterhood, brotherhood—perhaps for civility most of all.

The reflective executive is in short a hero and a saint, dressed in the ordinary garb of the marketplace. This executive is one who lives not only by getting things done but by getting the right things done because she lives in the sight of the Lord all days of her life. Her courage and her vision are unconquerable. She lives for her Master's counsel, and in his presence her heart is lifted up and consoled. She is anointed with the oil of gladness because she understands the generosity of the Lord's favor to her; and she is willing to walk through the canyons of cities built by commerce and weakened by double-dealing, to mend the broken statues, and to repair the shattered dreams.

Lord of the marketplace, I thank you for creating in me a heart sensitive to the needs of the whole human family; for giving me the creative apparatus to exercise executive leadership in your world of goods and services, of getting and spending, without, in the end, becoming estranged from you.

I stand in the center of Flushing Meadow Park, beside the metal globe that once stood at the center of a great World's Fair of countries and cultures. I remember the joy of creation spread out before us in a tapestry of exhibitions. The religions of the world, like the manufacturers of the world, the trade ministries of all the nations, were once gathered together here. In my mind's eye, I remember the metaphor of your creation I once saw in this space. I knew once, and can believe again, that great gatherings of the nations, whether in global church councils or global gatherings of nations come to market, can reveal your creativity, your heart, your will for humanity.

Lord of the marketplace, I thank you for the world vision you poured out on me then just as you poured out your word of prophecy to the nations. I rejoice in the charged energy of your presence in the action that transforms our hearts as we reach for a community of nations, a parliament of peace.

Lord of the marketplace, I ask that you give us the courage to believe in a day of reckoning, here or hereafter; something that calls us to account and demands that we become responsible; to cherish your people and your earth.

Open us, Lord, to the transformation of consciousness that only you can provide; teach us the way of your laws; empower us with your creative vision.

Lord, you are holy indeed, and all the marketplace rightly gives you praise.

Gerard Manley Hopkins had it right after all: the just woman justices. And by the streams of justice the righteous are consoled and refreshed for the task at hand. The cities that have been destroyed by the nihilists and the fools can be restored, can be built up again, if we have the heart and the will and the courage to do it. The forgiving minute is at hand, and Kipling's God has become a kinder fellow. When we see the things we spent our lives for broken, we can stoop and build them up with worn-out tools.

PRACTICUM

1. Write a prayer to the Lord of the marketplace. Share it with your colleagues.
2. Improve some lives, in whatever way lies within your power, through an initiative you believe in. Make the world a better place if you can.

THEMES FOR REFLECTION

The author proposed these themes for reflection at the Business Vocation Conference in Miami, Florida, held in May 1990 at the behest of Sysco executive Joseph Sciortino and the Archdiocese of Miami.

—A time to reflect on the definition of executive life as a response to needs, a process of discernment, a call to service
—A time to recognize the diversity of our personal calls and to realize unity in that diversity
—A time to remember the original dream that called us, the original vocational choice we made

—Further, a time to choose the work again, and in rechoosing the work to choose the Lord in the work
—To see the Lord walking ahead of us in the marketplace; to see God as Lord of the marketplace
—To understand the marketplace as a place of freedom; but where the competitive drive should not be selfishly guided
—A time to be conscious of sin
—A time to ask for a second naïveté
—A time to meditate on history as process; on Alfred North Whitehead's idea, "the creative advance into novelty;" to imagine God bringing new goodness to bear on old dilemmas; to pray to be part of it.

NOTES

Chapter 1: Effectiveness

1. Hannah Arendt, *The Human Condition* (Chicago and London: University of Chicago Press, 1958), p. 291.

2. William James, "Pragmatism's Conception of Truth," *Pragmatism and Other Essays* (New York: Washington Square Press, 1963), pp. 88–89.

3. Theodore Levitt, *The Marketing Imagination* (New York: Free Press, 1986), p. 226.

4. Ibid.

5. See Thomas S. Johnson, "Capitalism after Communism: Now Comes the Hard Part," as it appears in John Coleman, ed., *One Hundred Years of Catholic Social Thought*, (Maryknoll, N.Y.: Orbis Books, 1991), pp. 240–255.

6. Levitt, *The Marketing Imagination*, pp. 128–129.

7. Ibid.

8. See "Leap of Faith: Controversial Financing Plan Proposed as a Way to Salvage Junk-Bond Deal," by Tana Parker Pope, *Houston Chronicle*, August 30, 1992, p. 1A, 18A.

9. John Loudon, "Experiments in Truth," *Parabola*, Winter 1985, pp. 20, 21, 23.

10. C. S. Lewis, *Mere Christianity*, (New York: Macmillan, 1943; paperback edition, 1960), pp. 86–87.

11. Walt Whitman, *Leaves of Grass* (New York: Penguin Books, 1959—facsimile edition), p. 83.

Chapter 2: Time

1. Takeshi Umehara, "Eastern Minds Will Be Guiding World's Future," *Houston Chronicle*, August 30, 1992, p. 1F, 4F. Umehara is director general of the International Research Center in Kyoto.

2. William Barrett, *Irrational Man: A Study in Existential Philosophy* (Garden City, New York: Doubleday Anchor Books, 1958), p. 207.

3. Ibid.

4. Rudy Rucker, "Master of the Incomplete," *Science 82*, October, 1982, p. 59.

5. C. S. Lewis, "The Weight of Glory," as it appears in *The Weight of Glory, and Other Addresses*, revised and expanded edition, edited by Walter Hooper (New York: Macmillan, 1980), p. 18.

6. See Peter Drucker, *The Effective Executive* (New York: Harper & Row, 1966, 1967), Chap. 2, pp. 25–51.

7. Kathleen M. Eisenhardt, "Speed and Strategic Choice: How Managers Accelerate Decision-Making,"

paper given at the 1992 International Strategic Management Conference, New Orleans, manuscript p. 19.

Chapter 3: Contribution

1. Gerard Manley Hopkins, "As kingfishers catch fire," poem 34, line 8, as it appears in *Prose and Poems*, edited by W. H. Gardner (Harmondsworth, Middlesex, England: Penguin Books, 1953), p. 51.
2. Ibid., p. 67: poem 51, "Thou art indeed just, Lord," lines 3–4.
3. Personal interview with Phipps, as it appears in "Entrepreneurial Spirit: Greg Phipps," *Freeman Business* (publication of the A. B. Freeman School of Business, Tulane University, New Orleans, 1992), p. 3.
4. Stanley Marcus, *Quest for the Best* (New York: Viking Press, 1979), p. 145.
5. Ibid., pp. 145–146.
6. Ibid.
7. Ibid.

Chapter 4: Building on Strength

1. Evelyn Underhill, *The Spiritual Life* (New York: Harper & Row Publishers [no date]), p. 84.
2. Package copy, Kellogg's S.W. Graham Genuine Graham Cereal (Battle Creek, Mich.: Kellogg Company, 1988).
3. Transcript from videotape of commercial provided by Arnold Kirschman, president of Kirschman's.
4. Rosabeth Moss Kanter, *When Giants Learn to Dance: Mastering the Challenge of Strategy, Management, and Careers in the 1990s* (New York: Simon and Schuster, 1989), p. 13.

5. Ibid.
6. Ibid.
7. Ibid., p. 241.
8. See Bernard J. F. Lonergan, *Insight: A Study of Human Understanding* (New York: Philosophical Library, 1957), pp. 238–242.
9. Ibid.
10. Michael Novak, *Toward a Theology of the Corporation* (Washington, D.C.: American Enterprise Institute for Public Policy Research, 1981), p. 51.
11. "Potholes," *Vital Signs: An Anthology*, edited by Ronald Wallace (Madison, Wis.: University of Wisconsin Press, 1989), pp. 162–163.

Chapter 5: First Things First

1. Reminiscence of Arthur Howe, as quoted in "Egyptian battle of WWII forged bond between foes" by Mimi Mann, New Orleans *Times-Picayune*, October 18, 1992, p. A29.
2. See Os Guinness, *Winning Back the Soul of American Business* (Washington, D.C.: Hourglass Publishers, 1990), pp. 32–33.
3. Ibid., p. 33.
4. Ibid.
5. Drucker, *The Effective Executive*, p. 100.
6. See Wilfrid Desan, *The Planetary Man* (New York: Macmillan, 1972), p. 357.
7. Ibid., p. 358.
8. Ibid., p. 379.
9. Ibid.
10. Personal interview with Jordan, October 1992.
11. Desan, *The Planetary Man*, p. 38.

Chapter 6: Decision Making

1. Transcribed from audiotape of Napier Collyns speaking at the Planning Forum's 1992 International Strategic Management Conference, New Orleans, May 6.
2. Ibid.
3. Napier Collyns, as quoted in *The Deeper News: Exploring Future Business Environments*, Vol. 2, No. 4 (Summer 1991), p. 3.
4. Emily T. Smith, "The Next Trick for Business: Taking a Cue from Nature," *Business Week*, May 11, 1992, p. 74.
5. Ibid.
6. Ibid.

Chapter 7: Weighing Failure and Success

1. J. C. Penney, *View from the Ninth Decade: Jottings from a Merchant's Day-Book* (New York: Thomas Nelson, 1961), p. 116.
2. Ibid., p. 118.
3. Ibid.
4. Ibid., p. 120.
5. Ibid., p. 121.
6. Ibid., p. 122.
7. Ibid., p. 123.
8. Ibid., p. 125.
9. Ibid.
10. Ibid.
11. Ibid.
12. Ibid., p. 128.
13. Ibid.

Chapter 8: Lord of the Marketplace

1. See Bernard Lee and Michael Cowan, *Dangerous Memories: House Churches and Our American Story* (Kansas City, Kans.: Sheed & Ward, 1986), pp. 39 and following.

2. Here, and throughout this chapter, I am drawing on Dean Bausch's "The Context of Our Ministries," a working paper given under Jesuit auspices in 1981.

3. Robert S. McNamara, "Address to the Board of Governors 1976" (Washington, D.C.: The World Bank, 1976), as quoted in Lee Tavis's "Concepts of Professional Responsibility in Multinational Management Decisionmaking," a briefing paper delivered at IMC Annual Seminar, March 25, 1988, p. 5.

4. Bausch, "The Context of Our Ministries," p. 17.

5. Federico García Lorca, *Poet in New York*, translated by Greg Simon and Steven F. White, edited and with an Introduction and notes by Christopher Maurer (New York: Farrar, Straus & Giroux, 1988), p. 248.

6. Carl von Clausewitz, *On War* (London: Penguin, 1968), p. 341.

7. García Lorca, *Poet in New York*, p. 11.

SELECTED BIBLIOGRAPHY

Butt, Howard E., Jr. *The Velvet Covered Brick.* New York: Harper & Row, Publishers, 1973.

Coleman, John A., S.J. *One Hundred Years of Catholic Social Thought: Celebration and Challenge.* Maryknoll, New York: Orbis Books, 1991.

Colson, Chuck and Jack Eckerd. *Why America Doesn't Work.* Dallas: Word Publishing, 1992.

De Pree, Max. *Leadership Is an Art.* New York: Doubleday, 1989.

Desan, Wilfrid. *Let the Future Come: Perspectives for a Planetary Peace.* Volume III of *The Planetary Man.* Washington, D.C.: Georgetown University Press, 1987.

De Waal, Esther. *Living with Contradiction: Reflections on the Rule of St. Benedict.* San Francisco: Harper & Row, Publishers, 1989.

Diehl, William E. *The Monday Connection: A Spirituality of Competence, Affirmation, and Support in the Workplace.* San Francisco: HarperSanFrancisco, 1991.

Droel, William L. *Business People: The Spirituality of Work.* Chicago: ACTA Publications, 1990.

Duffy, Stephen J. *The Graced Horizon: Nature and Grace in Modern Catholic Thought.* Collegeville, Miss.: Michael Glazier Books, 1992.

Foster, Richard. *Money, Sex and Power: The Challenge of the Disciplined Life.* San Francisco: HarperSanFrancisco, 1985.

Green, Thomas H. *Darkness in the Marketplace: The Christian at Prayer in the World.* Notre Dame, Ind.: Ave Maria Press, 1981.

Guinness, Os. *Winning Back the Soul of American Business.* Washington, D.C.: Hourglass Publishers, 1990.

Haughey, John C. *Converting 9 to 5: A Spirituality of Daily Work.* New York: Crossroad, 1989.

———. *The Holy Use of Money: Personal Finances in Light of Christian Faith.* New York: Crossroad, 1989 (1986).

Holland, Joe. *Creative Communion: Toward a Spirituality of Work.* Mahwah, N.J.: Paulist Press, 1989.

Kaplan, Aryeh. *Jewish Meditation: A Practical Guide.* New York: Schocken Books, 1985.

Langan, John P. "Saints and Managers: The Challenge and Virtues of the Christian Business Leader," in

Discovering the Business Vocation: Proceedings of a National Conference, Washington, D.C., FADICA (Foundations and Donors Interested in Catholic Activities), 1990.

Lee, Bernard J. and Michael A. Cowan. *Dangerous Memories: House Churches and Our American Story.* Kansas City, Mo.: Sheed & Ward, 1986.

Lodahl, Michael E. *Shekinah Spirit: Divine Presence in Jewish and Christian Religion.* Mahwah, N.J.: Paulist Press, 1992.

Novak, Michael. *Toward a Theology of the Corporation.* Washington, D.C.: American Enterprise Institute for Public Policy Research, 1981.

Pierce, Gregory F. Augustine, ed. *Of Human Hands: A Reader in the Spirituality of Work.* Minneapolis: Augsburg, 1991. Chicago: ACTA Publications, 1991.

Schwartz, Peter. *The Art of the Long View.* New York: Doubleday Currency, 1991.

White, John. *Excellence in Leadership: Reaching Goals with Prayer, Courage, and Determination.* Downers Grove, Ill.: InterVarsity Press, 1986.